Set design by James Wolk

Photo by Susanne Richelle

Eevin Hartsough, Jeffrey Hayenga and Matthew Locricchio in a scene from the Philadelphia Festival Theatre for New Plays production of *Moon Over The Brewery*.

MOON OVER
THE BREWERY

BY BRUCE GRAHAM

★

DRAMATISTS
PLAY SERVICE
INC.

For
Amanda, Casey, Lindsay, Adam, Aric,
and all future nieces and nephews.

And thanks, to the town of Ashland, Pennsylvania.

MOON OVER THE BREWERY was produced at the Philadelphia Festival Theatre For New Plays (Dr. Carol Rocamora, Artistic and Producing Director) in Philadelphia, Pennsylvania, in April, 1989. It was directed by James J. Christy; the set design was by James Wolk; the costume design was by Vickie Esposito; the lighting design was by Karl Haas; the sound design was by Conny M. Lockwood; original paintings by Michael Wright Stockton; the production manager was Cynthia Hart and the stage manager was Paul Lockwood. The cast was as follows:

AMANDA WASLYK ....Eevin Hartsough
RANDOLPH...Jeffrey Hayenga
WARREN ZIMMERMAN ....Matthew Locricchio
MIRIAM WASLYK...Debra Monk

CHARACTERS

Amanda Waslyk
Randolph
Warren Zimmerman
Miriam Waslyk

THE SCENE

The action of the play takes place in and around the Waslyk
home, on the edge of a Pennsylvania coal town.

TIME

Spring. A couple years ago.

Act One:
Late afternoon.

Act Two:
Scene one: That evening.
Scene two: About two hours later.

"Who knows what true loneliness is ... to the lonely
themselves it wears a mask. The most miserable out-
cast hugs some memory or some illusion."
Joseph Conrad

MOON OVER THE BREWERY

ACT ONE

THE SCENE: The Waslyk home, somewhere in the coal regions of Pennsylvania. It's one of those houses you see sitting up on the side of the hill. To one side of the stage is the "front yard." An old rail fence is Upstage. On the other side is the actual house. There is a small open porch with a door leading to the living room. The Waslyk living room looks like an antique shop; it is filled with old things and various art projects. The dining room table is completely covered with various works-in-progress. To one side is a stairway leading upstairs, to the rear is a kitchen door. Prominently displayed, in a place of honor, is a beautiful quilt. There are lots of paintings ... all of them moonscapes. One sits on an easel, covered. It is late afternoon in April. Amanda Waslyk enters into the yard area. She is 13, but a very serious kid. Her clothes would be more suitable on an adult. She carries a briefcase and speaks over her shoulder as she enters.

AMANDA. *(Whispering urgently.)* Go away! It's not funny anymore. *(At the house, cautiously.)* Mother? You home? *(No answer. She turns offstage, this time speaking in a normal voice.)* Stop following me. *(Randolph strolls into view. He is of indeterminate age and wears a perfectly tailored white suit which could be slightly out of date, but it looks so good on him — who cares. Randolph is incredibly handsome. Cary Grant would be ideal casting, but we understand he's unavailable.)*
RANDOLPH. Women have such egos. You naturally assume I'm following you.
AMANDA. You are.
RANDOLPH. Perhaps I'm just out for a stroll.

7

AMANDA.   Up here?

RANDOLPH.   The strip mine is lovely in the spring.

AMANDA.   Go away.

RANDOLPH.   You've missed me.

AMANDA.   You wish.

RANDOLPH.   You have.

AMANDA.   You are so conceited, you know that?

RANDOLPH.   I've never had time for fake modesty.

AMANDA.   Go away. *(She heads for the front door.)*

RANDOLPH.   Don't you even want to know where I've been?

AMANDA.   No.

RANDOLPH.   Yes you do. You're dying for a good story.

AMANDA.   I'm serious — go away. You always get me in trouble.

RANDOLPH.   You need me.

AMANDA.   What for?

RANDOLPH.   You know. *(A beat.)*

AMANDA.   I don't need you and I don't want you here. And don't ever come to school again.

RANDOLPH.   *(Advancing on her.)* Who was that little toad with whom you were having such a serious conversation at the bus stop?

AMANDA.   He's not a toad.

RANDOLPH.   Peter, that's his name, isn't it?

AMANDA.   I hate it when you play games like this —

RANDOLPH.   Does Peter have a skin condition?

AMANDA.   He has a pimple —

RANDOLPH.   Sub-standard personal hygiene?

AMANDA.   All boys have them once in awhile.

RANDOLPH.   I never did.

AMANDA.   Well, you're perfect.

RANDOLPH.   After all these years you finally admit it. I should go away more often. *(She heads for the door; he blocks her way.)*

AMANDA.   Get out of my way.

RANDOLPH.   So what were you and the Elephant Man talking about?

AMANDA.   None of your business. *(She moves around him to the porch.)* Good-bye Randolph.

RANDOLPH. You need me. *(She turns to protest, but he beats her to it.)* Somebody was here last night.
AMANDA. *(Without conviction.)* No there wasn't.
RANDOLPH. Then why was I called away from such a fabulous party?
AMANDA. Nobody's stopping you. Go back to your party.
RANDOLPH. Didn't you hear someone laughing? Right around midnight?
AMANDA. That was the t.v.
RANDOLPH. Don't lie to me, m'love. I know you too well. *(He moves closely to her.)* Mother had that smile this morning. *(He takes out a cigarette case.)*
AMANDA. What smile?
RANDOLPH. You know. That Scarlett O'Hara-the-morning-after-Rhett-Butler-carried-her-up-the-stairs-smile. Cigarette? *(She shakes her head "no." He takes out a cigarette holder and proceeds to light up.)* Now think. When was the last time mother had anything resembling that smile? Four years ago. The ceramic tile salesman with a penchant for country music. If it wasn't for me we'd still be listening to songs about trucks.
AMANDA. I got rid of him — not you.
RANDOLPH. You're an amateur —
AMANDA. No I'm not —
RANDOLPH. Me — I'm the one who did it. I'm the person who saved you from having to ride in a car with large green dice hanging off the mirror.
AMANDA. *(Extending her hand.)* It's been a pleasure Randolph. Stop back again in four years. *(Again, he blocks her way.)*
RANDOLPH. What were you and this Peter talking about?
AMANDA. You're so smart, you tell me.
RANDOLPH. He was making some sort of indecent proposal, wasn't he?
AMANDA. He's thirteen.
RANDOLPH. That's when they start —
AMANDA. You're jealous, aren't you?
RANDOLPH. *(How absurd.)* Please ...
AMANDA. You are.
RANDOLPH. Of him? He's this big. *(He indicates a very short*

9

person.)

AMANDA.   No he's not. *(Randolph arches his eyebrows.)* He's still growing.

RANDOLPH.   He's a dwarf —

AMANDA.   Get out of my way —

RANDOLPH.   I adore you — *(This stops her.)*

AMANDA.   I know. *(She stares at him a moment.)* I'm taking French now.

RANDOLPH.   Really?

AMANDA.   Know how you say "I adore you" in French? *(Shakes his head.)* Je t'adore.

RANDOLPH.   Je t'adore. *(Silence.)* Tell me you've missed me.

AMANDA.   *(Quietly.)* Once in awhile.

RANDOLPH.   Because I've missed you —

AMANDA.   Now go away, please. She'll be home soon. *(He gets out of her way. She opens the door and enters the house.)*

RANDOLPH.   So this is how it ends, hmmm? Being abandoned for a midget with a growth on his face? *(Amanda looks at him a second, then laughs.)*

AMANDA.   You're a terrible martyr. *(Silence.)*

RANDOLPH.   I'm around whenever you need help getting rid of the midnight laugher. *(The phone rings.)* All you have to do is whistle. You do know how to whistle don't you?

AMANDA.   Get an original line, okay Randolph?

RANDOLPH.   You're right. It's better when Bacall says it. *(He blows her a kiss.)* I'm around. *(She crosses the living room and answers the phone. Randolph moves out of her view, but remains on the porch.)*

AMANDA.   Hello Mrs. Simpers ... I just knew it was you ... no, I told you I wouldn't know anything until after four ... the latest offer still stands at thirteen hundred dollars ... I can't tell you who the other bidder is ... *(She plops into a chair, taking off her shoes.)* No, mother's not home yet ... it wouldn't make any difference ... my mother never talks business — that's why she had me ... okay, get back to me with a figure. *(She hangs up, smiles. She enjoyed that. She crosses to the kitchen — stops — sees a note hanging on the door, takes it down and reads it. She lets out a little sigh of disgust.)*

10

RANDOLPH. *(From the porch.)* I said whistle, not sigh. *(She moves right to him, not surprised that he's still there.)*

AMANDA. *(Indicating the note.)* Someone's coming for dinner.

RANDOLPH. Really?

AMANDA. *(Nodding.)* She wants me to set the floor.

RANDOLPH. *(Reading over her shoulder.)* Who's the honored guest?

AMANDA. Doesn't say.

RANDOLPH. Care to venture a guess, Old Sport? The midnight laugher perhaps.

AMANDA. Who knows.

RANDOLPH. My, he moves fast.

AMANDA. We don't know for sure —

RANDOLPH. Things are kind of reversed though, aren't they? Isn't it customary to dine together first and then spend the night?

AMANDA. *(Sharp.)* Randolph!

RANDOLPH. *(Chastised.)* That was uncalled for.

AMANDA. You always find the dirt in things.

RANDOLPH. Everyone needs a hobby.

AMANDA. It was the t.v. ... I heard the t.v.

RANDOLPH. Whatever you say — *(Amanda begins to clear a place on the floor.)*

AMANDA. *(Convincing herself.)* If someone was here why didn't I see something this morning? We always knew when Morty stayed.

RANDOLPH. Perhaps this one doesn't use Aqua Velva. *(She begins to move a stack of canvasses.)*

AMANDA. It's just a dinner — that's all.

RANDOLPH. *(Looking at the canvasses.)* Doesn't she ever get tired of moonscapes?

AMANDA. Why should she?

RANDOLPH. Kind of limits your use of color. *(He crosses to the easel.)* This the new one?

AMANDA. Yes.

RANDOLPH. May I? *(She moves to the easel, lifting the cover from the painting.)* What part of town is that?

AMANDA. I don't know. *(She looks closer.)* Looks like she's

11

facing ... Beertown. See? That's the brewery.

RANDOLPH.   Beertown. She's slumming. *(She observes it.)*

AMANDA.   I like it. *(She covers it back up and resumes clearing the area.)*

RANDOLPH.   I really don't enjoy being a pest, but we should start plotting some sort of strategy.

AMANDA.   What for?

RANDOLPH.   Our dinner guest. It's been a few years — we're out of practice.

AMANDA.   Stop it —

RANDOLPH.   We're a team here Old Sport. And when it comes to intruders we're batting a thousand. Now, I suggest ground glass in the ice cream —

AMANDA.   We don't even know he's the one coming for dinner —

RANDOLPH.   Ahh-hahh! You admit there was a "he" here. *(She starts to answer back — stops)*

AMANDA.   I've got paint on my hands. *(She heads for the stairs; he steps in front of her.)*

RANDOLPH.   How many have there been, anyway?

AMANDA.   I don't know —

RANDOLPH.   There was that one when you were very little. You know ... the prince of polyester ... what was his name?

AMANDA.   Bill.

RANDOLPH.   Right, Bill. How could I forget such an exotic name. Then there was Steve —

AMANDA.   You're in my way again —

RANDOLPH.   Remember Steve? The truck driver who lived to spit. Delightful chap, as long as you kept him outside.

AMANDA.   Randolph ...

RANDOLPH.   And Morty, the country music fan. A lover of women who sing through their noses —

AMANDA.   You're getting on my nerves —

RANDOLPH.   That's three. And all of them ... gone. With my help, of course.

AMANDA.   *(Holding out her hands.)* Out of my way or I smear this all over your suit. *(Randolph gets out of her way; she exits up the stairs.)*

RANDOLPH. We're 3-0 Old Sport. And you know I hate to lose. *(The quilt catches his eye.)* My God, that is beautiful.

AMANDA. *(Off.)* What?

RANDOLPH. *(He moves to pick it up.)* This quilt.

AMANDA. *(Off.)* Don't touch it. That's my ticket to New York. I'm getting ten percent for that and I've got to get her up to thirteen hundred dollars.

RANDOLPH. My God, who has that kind of money around here?

AMANDA. Guess.

RANDOLPH. Mrs. Simpers.

AMANDA. That's right.

RANDOLPH. She is a vile woman —

AMANDA. But her checks are just fine. And as soon as I get her up to 1300 dollars I'll take my percentage and pay for the school trip.

RANDOLPH. I really don't like the idea of something this lovely wrapped around someone like her. It's too big of a contradiction. *(Amanda enters to the top of the stairs. She stands a moment, then walks down, looking grim.)*

AMANDA. Guess what I just found on the edge of the tub. *(He shrugs; she holds out a man's wristwatch.)*

RANDOLPH. A Timex.

AMANDA. Do you believe that?

RANDOLPH. Not even a top of the line Timex —

AMANDA. How could she do this? Here I am, willing to give her the benefit of the doubt and ... and she snuck a man in here. She's never done anything like that before —

RANDOLPH. As far as we know —

AMANDA. I mean, she always brought them home so we could go through the whole charade of meeting them and everything. But ... I mean — to sneak a man in here so that she could ... *(She looks over at him. Simultaneously, they do an identical "ecchhhh ..." sound, indicating their displeasure.)*

RANDOLPH. I think it's time you sat your mother down and had a very stern talk with her.

AMANDA. It's so dishonest. I mean, I know she's a little goofy sometimes, but she's always honest.

RANDOLPH. I think we may have a problem here. *(He moves away from her; she follows.)*

AMANDA. What?

RANDOLPH. Let's face it: when it comes to men your mother is not exactly a gourmet. She's more into fast food.

AMANDA. Get to the point —

RANDOLPH. Look at her resumé, m'love. It's a long line of losers and slobs.

AMANDA. *(Sharply.)* Except my father.

RANDOLPH. *(Softening.)* Of course. An intelligent, sensitive man. And a good dresser. But let's face it Amanda, he was a fluke.

AMANDA. So.

RANDOLPH. So if she went to all the trouble to introduce us to the three stooges ... why would she feel compelled to sneak this one in? *(Amanda sits, allowing this to sink in. From offstage, Warren Zimmerman enters. He wears a summer mailman's uniform, complete with shorts and knee socks.)*

AMANDA. My God ... you're probably right. *(Warren looks up at the house.)*

RANDOLPH. Don't be at all surprised if our dinner guest turns out to be a leper in a bowling shirt.

WARREN. Hello? *(They both jump, startled, then scurry to the window and peek through the drapes.)*

RANDOLPH. Even worse. A mailman.

WARREN. Hello? Anybody home?

AMANDA. A mailman ...

RANDOLPH. Well, at least he can read. *(Warren stands at the edge of the stage, looking a bit reluctant to proceed. He is in his early 40's, a few pounds overweight, and carries a mailbag. He gives himself the once over, making sure everything is tucked in. Amanda and Randolph whisper urgently.)*

AMANDA. She's slipping. At least Steve had a nice body.

RANDOLPH. There's a paradox for you. If walking is such good exercise, why are there so many fat mailmen?

AMANDA. What does he want?

RANDOLPH. Dinner?

AMANDA. It's too early —

14

RANDOLPH.   Appetizers then — I don't know ...
WARREN.   Hello? *(He crosses towards the porch.)*
AMANDA.   *(To herself.)* Go away ... please go away ...
RANDOLPH.   Should I take care of him?
AMANDA.   You're not even supposed to be here —
RANDOLPH.   He's on the porch —
AMANDA.   Shhh ...
RANDOLPH.   If only we had a vat of molten iron upstairs —
(Warren knocks on the door.)
WARREN.   Hello?
RANDOLPH.   Where's the gun? You're thirteen and all alone
— no jury would convict you —
AMANDA.   Shhh ...
WARREN.   Anybody home? *(Very tentatively, he begins to open
the screendoor.)*
RANDOLPH.   He's coming in — do something! *(Randolph
shoves her into the doorway.)*
AMANDA.   Yes?
WARREN.   Oh my God! *(He is obviously startled and backs off the
porch, catching his breath. Amanda stands in the doorway, calm;
Randolph remains inside. Out of breath.)* I'm ... I'm ... I'm ...
AMANDA.   You're not going to die or anything are you?
WARREN.   I don't ... I don't usually go into ... people's houses
... like that. Just startled.
AMANDA.   Our mailbox is down on the road. *(She begins to
shut the door.)*
WARREN.   I know. *(He moves onto the porch.)* I'm not the
mailman. I mean, not your mailman.
AMANDA.   Then what do you want? *(A beat. He laughs nerv-
ously.)*
WARREN.   Well ... tell you the truth, I'm not sure. You don't
know me, at least I don't think so —
AMANDA.   Could we get to the point sometime today? I have
homework.
RANDOLPH.   My, aren't we subtle ...
WARREN.   Well, uhh ... my name is Warren and I'm a friend
of your mom's —
RANDOLPH.   "Friend." Creative euphemism.

WARREN. And uhh ... well, I'm coming over for dinner to-
night. I don't know whether she told you or not. *(He waits for
a reaction. None comes. She is too busy motioning for Randolph to
shut up.)* Did she?
AMANDA. Did she what?
WARREN. Tell you. About me.
AMANDA. Should she have?
RANDOLPH. Slowly m'love ... slowly ...
WARREN. Well, it's kind of last minute. She may have forgot-
ten.
AMANDA. Yes. Women her age often do that. *(Warren is
unsure how to react, then laughs.)*
WARREN. Look, why don't we start over again. Hi, I'm
Warren —
AMANDA. What's your last name?
WARREN. Zimmerman.
RANDOLPH. Warren Zimmerman?
WARREN. And you must be Amanda Waslyk.
RANDOLPH. Warrennnnnn Zimmermannnnnnn ...
AMANDA. Yes —
RANDOLPH. Sounds like a beehive —
WARREN. Well, I'm your dinner guest for this evening. *(He
extends his hand. Amanda remains inside.)* Nice to meet you.
AMANDA. I'm not supposed to open the door to strangers.
RANDOLPH. Weak ... very weak ...
WARREN. Oh, sure. *(He backs away.)*
RANDOLPH. Lighten up. He's getting frightened.
AMANDA. You understand. I mean, I don't really know you.
WARREN. No, of course. Your mom's right: don't go lettin'
strangers in the house — absolutely right. *(He pulls wine from
mailbag.)* I just wanted to drop off some wine.
RANDOLPH. Don't let him get away yet. We need ammuni-
tion.
AMANDA. Will you shutup?
WARREN. Beg your pardon?
AMANDA. Nothing.
WARREN. I'm sorry ... do you have company?
AMANDA. No.

16

WARREN. Sounded like you were talking to someone. *(She shakes her head. He puts two bottles of wine — one red, one white — on the steps.)* Well, I just wanted to drop these off for dinner. *(He looks about to leave.)*

RANDOLPH. Stop him. *(She steps out onto the porch; Randolph follows. At no time does Warren acknowledge Randolph.)*

AMANDA. Have you known my mother long?

WARREN. *(A little surprised.)* Quite awhile.

AMANDA. Really?

WARREN. Five years at least. *(He observes her.)* You're outside.

RANDOLPH. *(Circling Warren, observing.)* Brilliant.

WARREN. *(Smiling.)* Figure you can trust me?

AMANDA. You look harmless —

RANDOLPH. Not to mention vacuous —

WARREN. I'm not sure whether that's a compliment or not.

RANDOLPH. It's not.

AMANDA. How do you know my mother?

WARREN. From the diner. She's been servin' me my lunch for ... long time now. 'Fact, I used to eat right at noon, but the diner's nuts then, so now I eat at two thirty when it's nice and quiet. That way we get a chance to talk. *(A beat. Amanda says nothing.)* Your mother's a terrific waitress.

AMANDA. She's an artist too you know.

WARREN. Yes, I —

AMANDA. And she went to college. She didn't graduate, but she went.

RANDOLPH. Methinks the lady dost protest too much....

WARREN. Yes, I know. But ... uhh, well there's nothing wrong with being a waitress.

RANDOLPH. Another one with no ambition. What is that woman's problem?

AMANDA. She's never mentioned you.

WARREN. Well, there's really not a lot to mention. I'm just ... sorta there.

RANDOLPH. Low self esteem. This'll be a breeze. *(Warren picks up the bottles.)*

WARREN. Would you mind sticking these in the icebox? That way they'll be cold for dinner.

AMANDA. *(Looking at the bottles.)* You're not supposed to chill a cabernet.

WARREN. Shows how much I know. I put ice cubes in it. *(He laughs; she stares.)*

RANDOLPH. Lighten up. *(She laughs along with him.)* Now, invite him in.

AMANDA. *(To Randolph.)* What?

WARREN. Nothing.

AMANDA. *(To Warren.)* What?

WARREN. Nothing. You said "what?" and I said nothing because I hadn't said anything.

RANDOLPH. Don't pursue it Old Sport. *(Randolph heads for the door. She turns as he does.)*

WARREN. *(Observing her.)* Are you okay?

AMANDA. Yes.

RANDOLPH. Invite him in. We'll start round one. *(Starting to leave.)*

WARREN. Well ... it was nice to meet you —

RANDOLPH. Now!

AMANDA. Would you like to come in for a minute? *(Warren stops — surprised.)*

WARREN. What about the no stranger rule?

AMANDA. You're Warren Zimmerman, you're a mailman, you eat at the diner. See? You're not officially a stranger. *(She opens the door. Randolph enters.)* Come on in if you want.

WARREN. Okay. Thanks. *(He follows her in.)*

AMANDA. Can I get you something? I'll open one of these bottles if you have a drinking problem and wanted to get started early. *(Warren laughs.)*

RANDOLPH. *(Observing.)* He's too dumb to be insulted.

WARREN. A glass of water'd be nice.

AMANDA. What kind?

WARREN. I have a choice?

AMANDA. Tonic, seltzer, tap or mountain spring?

WARREN. Whatever's open. *(She exits into the kitchen. Warren proceeds to inspect the artwork as Randolph inspects Warren.)*

RANDOLPH. You're out of practice m'love. You're going directly for the jugular. Remember the treatment. Lull him, let him get comfortable. His defenses drop — then you nail him. Back off, repeat procedure. Like at the dentist's office: pastels and bland music to get you all relaxed, and then ... *(He makes a thrusting movement.)* He stabs you. *(Amanda enters with water.)* Remember: pain is always sharper when it's least expected.

AMANDA. Mountain spring.

WARREN. Thanks. Your mom's some artist.

AMANDA. Yes.

WARREN. And she does a little bit of everything. She paints, she sculpts ...

AMANDA. Short attention span. *(Randolph clears his throat. Amanda laughs, meaning the last comment was a joke.)*

WARREN. Does she ever do anything besides moonscapes?

AMANDA. Just once. A portrait of me when I was four.

WARREN. Can I see it?

AMANDA. No.

WARREN. Why not?

AMANDA. Because it's accurate. I was not a cute child.

RANDOLPH. But you're a ravishing young woman. *(She smiles at Randolph.)*

WARREN. Well, I really like her paintings. "Moon over Dorfman's Hardware Store" — that's my favorite.

AMANDA. Where did you see that?

WARREN. The diner. She has a couple of them hanging by the register.

AMANDA. I wish she wouldn't do that.

WARREN. That place needs all the help it can get.

AMANDA. A layer of grease and cigar smoke doesn't enhance the value.

WARREN. But at least people get to see them. *(He begins to look through the other canvasses.)* I mean, if you keep them up here to yourself, no one gets to enjoy them. What's the point of creating them?

AMANDA. Warren, we're not talking art appreciation here; we're talking about money. *(Warren looks at her a second, then starts to laugh.)*

RANDOLPH. He's laughing. Why is he laughing? *(To Amanda.)* Why is he laughing?

AMANDA. *(Calmly.)* Something funny?

WARREN. No ... I just.... *(He attempts to stop, but starts all over again.)*

RANDOLPH. He's mentally unstable. We should've known by the socks.

WARREN. This is rude of me I know. It's just ... well, I laugh at ... strange or ... inappropriate times.

RANDOLPH. Like midnight?

WARREN. It's just that ... you're just like your mother described you.

AMANDA. What did she say?

WARREN. Oh, just that you were very serious. She calls you the young Republican.

RANDOLPH. That's better than when she called you the Bad Seed —

WARREN. The two of you are so different. Your mother's such a ...

RANDOLPH. Flake?

AMANDA. Free spirit?

WARREN. Yeah, I guess. She's so ... different.

AMANDA. It's okay Warren, you can call her eccentric if you want.

RANDOLPH. Everyone else does.

WARREN. Well, I think most people want artists to be different.

AMANDA. Why?

RANDOLPH. He's relaxing. Get ready to pounce.

WARREN. Well, most of us lead kinda ... — I don't want to say "dull" but — quiet, I guess. Most of us lead kind of quiet lives and it's sort of fun to be with people who are more ... colorful. Dontcha think?

RANDOLPH. Go!

AMANDA. Do you have to start every sentence with "well"?

WARREN. Do I?

AMANDA. *(Nodding.)* I've known you ten minutes now and you've prefaced almost every sentence with "well." Now does this give you time to gather your thoughts or just a nervous habit? *(A beat. He smiles.)*

WARREN. Well, I never really thought about it. *(She starts to react.)* That was on purpose.

RANDOLPH. He got you ...

AMANDA. It's just that things like that tend to drive me nuts. Like kids at school who always say "Ya know." Of course I know, they don't have to keep telling me. Doesn't that bother you? *(He starts to respond — stops.)* What's the matter?

WARREN. I almost said, "Well, no." See that? You've got me paranoid.

RANDOLPH. Good. Step one complete. *(Warren begins to move around the room.)*

WARREN. I had this landlord one time — when I lived out in the desert — and he always said, "Know what I mean?" And he would use it when it made no sense like ... "Pass the salt, know what I mean?" *(He looks to her for a reaction.)*

RANDOLPH. He's nervous; calm him down. *(She laughs.)*

AMANDA. Why were you living in the desert?

WARREN. *(Shrugging.)* Just ended up there one day. Got a job in a museum.

AMANDA. Really?

WARREN. Well, don't get too impressed. It was the Roy Rogers Museum. *(Catches himself.)* Opps. Did it again.

AMANDA. What?

WARREN. Said "well."

AMANDA. I'll survive. *(Honestly interested.)* There's a Roy Rogers Museum?

WARREN. Oh yeah. It's quite popular.

AMANDA. What could they possibly have in the Roy Rogers Museum? *(Warren moves to within close proximity of wherever Amanda has left his watch. He does not see it.)*

RANDOLPH. He's going to find the watch. We need that watch.

WARREN. Stuffed animals mostly. Trigger, Bullet the dog ... *(He stops.)* You do know who Roy Rogers was don't you?

AMANDA. *(Patronizing.)* Yes.

WARREN. Right, dumb question. Your mom told me — you're an old movie freak. You're probably the only person your age who knows who Roy Rogers was. Which reminds me, I brought you a present. *(He turns to get his mailbag and Amanda lunges for the watch. He turns as she does this. Smiling.)* Don't be so anxious. Not that great a present.

RANDOLPH. Way to go. *(Warren pulls a bag from the pouch.)*

AMANDA. You didn't have to bring me anything.

WARREN. Well, I brought your mom the wine and — *(He stops.)* Did it again.

AMANDA. Warren, stopping and acknowledging it is even more annoying than saying it.

WARREN. Okay. *(Hands her the package.)* Didn't have time to wrap it. I'm lousy at it anyway.

RANDOLPH. Watch it — it's a bribe. *(She pulls out a book.)*

WARREN. The Encyclopedia of Film. *(He laughs.)* I always do that. I give someone a present and then I announce what it is. Like you were blind or something. *(She glances at Randolph, showing him the book.)* I did it with my mother one time. She opened this box and I yelled, "Towels!", and then I realized I'd given her the wrong box. It was a bathrobe. She looked at me like I was an idiot.

AMANDA. Thank you.

RANDOLPH. *(Not liking her tone.)* You can't be bought for $24.95. *(Warren reaches into the pouch.)* Now. *(She places the bag on top of his watch.)*

WARREN. *(Handing her another.)* One more.

AMANDA. *Shogun?*

WARREN. Have you read it?

AMANDA. I never read anything they can make into a mini-series.

WARREN. It's a terrific story.

AMANDA. I tend to prefer more ... literary oriented novels.

RANDOLPH. Ohh ... awkwardly phrased.

WARREN. You ought to give yourself a break once in awhile. Otherwise it's sort of like ... broccoli. *(She stares at him.)*

AMANDA. How so?

RANDOLPH. This should be interesting.

WARREN. Well, I mean ... brocolli's supposed to be so good for ya, right? But whatta you gonna do — spend your whole life eating nothin' but broccoli. *(Shaking his head.)* Once in awhile, everybody needs a bag of Doritos. *(A beat.)*

RANDOLPH. Oh my God ...

WARREN. *(Pointing to the book.)* Give it a try.

AMANDA. Maybe when I finish *The Great Gatsby.*

RANDOLPH. Don't ever finish that one. I look great in this wardrobe. *(The phone rings.)*

WARREN. I wasn't sure what to get you. Your mom says you love to read, but from what she told me I figured you weren't the Nancy Drew type. *(Rings again.)* Aren't you going to answer that?

AMANDA. No.

WARREN. Oh. *(A beat.)* Look, if it's a private call or something I can step outside.

AMANDA. It's not private. *(Rings again. Warren looks uncomfortable.)* Something wrong?

WARREN. Maybe I'm old fashioned but ... when a phone rings, I answer it. Habit I guess.

RANDOLPH. *(Smiling at Warren's discomfort.)* This is kind of fun. *(Rings again.)*

WARREN. Doesn't that drive you nuts?

AMANDA. No.

WARREN. You're not curious?

AMANDA. It's Mrs. Simpers.

WARREN. *The* Mrs. Simpers?

AMANDA. *(Nodding.)* And that was her last ring. *(They wait a moment. No ring.)*

WARREN. Very good.

AMANDA. Easy. She's been calling a couple times a day. Always five rings.

WARREN. How do you know her?

AMANDA. I don't. Every few months she sends her maid around to see what she can buy.

WARREN. Elvira or Mary Lou? I'd guess Mary Lou. *(Amanda nods.)* Mrs. Simpers doesn't like Elvira to use the car anymore. She has this habit of waving to people as she's driving and turning the wheel in the same direction. It's a friendly gesture, but the people usually end up running away screaming.

RANDOLPH. This man is a fountain of useless information.

AMANDA.   How'd you know?

WARREN.   I'm the local mailman. I know everything.

AMANDA.   Have you met Mrs. Simpers?

WARREN.   *(Nodding.)* She used to be on my route. Why don't you answer her phone call?

AMANDA.   Making her squirm. It's all part of the negotiating process. *(He looks blank.)* She wants to buy that quilt. *(She points. He moves to it.)* I told her I'd give her an answer today, but I still have to get her up another two hundred dollars.

WARREN. Your mom told me about this. She's been working on it forever. *(He picks it up.)*

RANDOLPH.   Oh sure. Let him touch it. *(She shoots him a "shutup" look. He moves to the stairs and sits.)*

WARREN.   *(Examining it.)* Ahh, here it is. *(Shows her.)* This piece of material. I gave it to your mom. *(Looks further.)* And this one here.

RANDOLPH.   Tell him no percentage.

WARREN.   They were from my mother's dresses.

AMANDA.   Doesn't she mind you making big holes in them?

WARREN.   Well ... she passed away about a year ago.

RANDOLPH.   Say you're sorry.

AMANDA.   I'm sorry.

WARREN.   Thank you. *(He puts the quilt down — touches it.)* I really admire your mom ...

RANDOLPH.   Here it comes again.

WARREN.   I mean, all her talents ... *(Points to the easel.)* Is that the new one?

AMANDA.   Yes. You can look at it if you want.

WARREN.   No ... no. That's my birthday present.

RANDOLPH.   She's giving them away again.

WARREN.   Today's my birthday.

RANDOLPH. Say happy birthday —

AMANDA.   Happy birthday.

WARREN.   Thank you.

AMANDA.   You're not going to make me guess your age are you? I can't stand when people do that. You always have to guess a few years younger than you really think just to be polite.

WARREN.   No secret. I'm 44.

RANDOLPH.   *(Not snide, honest.)* He's old.

WARREN.   Your mom knows I love her paintings, so she said she'd do one of the brewery. I'm from Beertown over there — I live right next to it.

RANDOLPH.   And all this time I thought it was his cologne.

WARREN.   *(Observing Amanda's reaction.)* Ahh, you just gave me the "Beertown look" and I'll bet you didn't even realize it.

AMANDA.   What's that?

WARREN.   Whenever you tell people you're from Beertown they always look as if they want to lock up all the valuables.

AMANDA.   It's not the best part of town.

WARREN.   It's got it's good points. Like, where my house is; it's sort of catty corner to the brewery. And there are these huge windows in the part where they store the empty bottles and in the spring the sun hits it in the afternoon — and they've got the brown bottles and the green bottles, you know — and the light turns it into one huge ... prism. Lights up the whole street. And it changes everyday. Some afternoons I come home, put my feet up on the porch and just stare at it.

RANDOLPH.   Now there's something to enhance the property value.

AMANDA.   *(Aiming up the stairs at Randolph.)* Shhh ... *(Warren turns, catching her.)* What?

WARREN.   Look Amanda, if you got some friends over after school ... I mean, don't feel like you have to hide them or anything.

AMANDA.   *(Evasive.)* What do you mean?

RANDOLPH.   You blew it Old Sport.

WARREN.   If your mom doesn't want you to have friends over when she's not here well ... that's between you guys. I won't say anything. *(She crosses towards him.)*

RANDOLPH.   Don't trust him.

AMANDA.   So ... if I had a friend here ... you wouldn't tell my mother ...

WARREN.   *(Hesitant.)* As long as you're not plannin' on burnin' down the house or anything. Then I feel I'd have to say something.

AMANDA. But you promise not to. Right? You promise?

WARREN. Mailman's honor. *(Randolph snorts.)* Okay?

AMANDA. Okay.

WARREN. And they don't have to hide upstairs. I'd like to meet them —

AMANDA. She's doing her homework.

WARREN. Oh.

RANDOLPH. *(Insulted.)* She? *(Warren looks at the quilt again.)*

WARREN. You know, maybe this is none of my business, but your mom doesn't really want to sell that quilt —

RANDOLPH. Zing him!

AMANDA. Why are you a mailman? *(A beat.)*

WARREN. Your ... train of thought's a little hard to follow sometimes.

AMANDA. *(Ignoring this.)* Did you grow up wanting to be one, or what?

WARREN. *(Smiling.)* I don't think any kid grows up really wanting to be a mailman. After I got out of the army I bummed around — I think I told you that — and I was working down in the Everglades with this guy who wrestled alligators. I'd take tickets, do the announcing — actually replaced him one time when he was in jail —

RANDOLPH. He's making this up —

AMANDA. You wrestled an alligator?

WARREN. Didn't take a lot of courage. It was about eighty years old with maybe nine teeth and they fed it a bottle of bourbon before every show to keep it mellow.

AMANDA. You really did that?

WARREN. Sure. And it's not easy workin' with a drunk alligator. I had to make sure it stayed awake while I was supposed to be wrestling it.

AMANDA. *(Laughing.)* But that's so ... stupid. *(They both laugh. Warren seems relaxed for a moment.)*

RANDOLPH. Stop it! *(She stops suddenly. Warren notices.)*

WARREN. You got me sidetracked. Anyway, I was working down there when I got a call that my father had died.

RANDOLPH. Say you're sorry —

AMANDA. I'm sorry.

26

WARREN. Thank you. Well, anyway, I came home — naturally — and it was kind of strange. My father and I hadn't even spoken since my divorce ...

RANDOLPH. This should be good. More ammo — more ammo....

AMANDA. You were married?

WARREN. Long time ago.

AMANDA. Why'd you get divorced? *(Warren looks at her a moment, surprised by the question. He begins to laugh.)*

RANDOLPH. What is the matter with this man?

WARREN. Sorry ... it's that ... inappropriate laughter I was telling you about. *(He calms down.)* Ahh ... well, that's a good question. Tell ya the truth, I'm not sure.

RANDOLPH. Never trust anyone who says "Tell ya the truth."

WARREN. We were 19 when we got married and then I got drafted. When I got out we were 24 and ... well ... *(He shrugs.)* Things change. People change. *(Suddenly.)* I didn't beat her or anything, if that's what you're worried about.

AMANDA. *(Cooly.)* Why should I be worried about that? *(A beat. He is awkward.)*

WARREN. Right.

RANDOLPH. Well played m'love.

WARREN. I got sidetracked again. *(He thinks.)* Right, so I came back for the funeral and realized that ... mom was getting older and ... I decided to stick around here for awhile. And since I had to get a job — and I was going to be staying put for awhile — I figured I better find something I wanted to do. So I sat down one day and I made up a list of all the things I really liked in life, and then I'd try and find a job that had some of those things in it. And ... uhh, well, I like being outside, I like to go for walks, I like ... people. And dogs —like dogs. *(Proudly.)* I have never had a problem with a dog on my route. Never. Some of the guys down the post office go out like Sylvester Stallone, you know, with the mace and everything. Not me. I get along fine with dogs.

RANDOLPH. That looks good on the resumé. *(Amanda shoots him a look.)*

WARREN. So, I went over my list —

RANDOLPH. Don't give me that look.

WARREN. And became a mailman. 'Course I also wrote down drinkin' a few beers and goin' fishin', but there aren't a lot of job opportunities for those sorta' skills. Between us, I can do my whole route in three hours, but I have to stay out the whole time so ... I talk to people. I have pictures of them in an album. Well, not all of them, just the ones I'm close to. Maybe you'd like to see it sometime?

RANDOLPH. Now there's an evening. *(Amanda shoots Randolph another look.)*

WARREN. I know, it probably sounds pretty dull —

RANDOLPH. *(To Amanda.)* What is your problem?

WARREN. But there are some pretty interesting people in this town if you know where to look. *(Warren notices she is distracted.)* So ... that's why I'm a mailman. And if it wasn't for January and February, and these knee socks they make us wear, I'd say it was just about a perfect job. *(She is still intent on Randolph. Warren stands.)* Well, I better get goin'. I've been ... kind of runnin' at the mouth here.

AMANDA. *(Absently.)* Okay. *(He moves towards the door.)*

WARREN. Gotta get cleaned up for dinner. *(He stands at the door. Extends his hand.)* Nice to meet you Amanda.

RANDOLPH. Go ahead. Shake his paw.

AMANDA. Nice to meet you. *(They shake.)*

WARREN. See you tonight. *(He steps out, putting on his pouch.)*

AMANDA. Thank you for the books.

RANDOLPH. I didn't tell you to say that.

WARREN. You're welcome. *(He waves, and starts to leave.)*

RANDOLPH. *(Whispering urgently.)* The watch. Get the watch!

AMANDA. Not now.

RANDOLPH. He's comfortable. Zing him!

AMANDA. Later —

RANDOLPH. Now! *(She does not react.)* Do it Amanda ... *(She picks up the watch as Warren is about to exit.)*

AMANDA. Warren?

WARREN. *(Stopping.)* Yeah?

AMANDA. Would you happen to know what time it is?

WARREN. Oh sure, it's ... *(On reflex he looks at his wrist. There is no watch. He looks back up at her, embarrassed. She holds out his watch.)* Uhhh ... listen Amanda ... I think I ought to ... *(She tosses it to him. He catches it.)*

AMANDA.   See you tonight Warren. *(She steps back inside, shutting the door. He stands there a moment, unsure, then exits. Amanda watches from the window. She turns to Randolph, who applauds.)* You're easily amused —

RANDOLPH.   And you're getting soft. What's the matter with you?

AMANDA.   Why do you have to rush things?

RANDOLPH.   He's a dolt —

AMANDA.   He's not that bad —

RANDOLPH.   For God's sake m'love: the man stares at beer bottles! *(Leaning into her.)* We don't need him here! If you didn't want me to get rid of him, why'd you call me?

AMANDA.   I didn't call you — you just showed up.

RANDOLPH.   Well as long as I'm here could you mix me a drink?

AMANDA.   A quick one. She should've been home by now. *(She enters the kitchen.)*

RANDOLPH.   I'll handle your mother.

AMANDA.   *(Off.)* You just leave, okay? I've seen my mother really mad three times in my life and two of them had to do with you. *(She enters carrying two champagne glasses and a can of 7 Up.)* I mean it Randolph. Take off when she gets here.

RANDOLPH.   What's the difference? She'll know about me sooner or later.

AMANDA.   Not if you go away —

RANDOLPH.   You don't think the mailman's going to keep our secret, do you?

AMANDA.   He said he would —

RANDOLPH.   He's a grown up! They always stick together on these things.

AMANDA.   *(Defiant.)* I don't think he'll tell.

RANDOLPH.   Suit yourself. You know how much I enjoy saying "I told you so." *(She puts his glass on the table and walks away with hers.)*

AMANDA.   There's your drink.

RANDOLPH.   And what was that fake fascination about? *(He reaches for his drink, but an old sword catches his eye.)*
AMANDA.   I was being polite —
RANDOLPH.   We better start planning our strategy — *(Picking up the sword.)* This might come in handy.
AMANDA.   You're not going to be here —
RANDOLPH.   *(Fencing.)* What say I challenge him to a duel, hmmm? For your mother's honor. Of course I'm a few hours too late.
AMANDA.   Put that back.
RANDOLPH.   *(Returning it to table.)* Where did she get something like this anyway?
AMANDA.   Garage sale. She's trying to branch into antique sales.
RANDOLPH.   Another Miriam Waslyk losing enterprise —
AMANDA.   She's going to be home in a minute —
RANDOLPH.   *(Ignoring her.)* I've got it. Directly after dinner we'll play the encyclopedia game. Warren looks easily humiliated —
AMANDA.   No — no encyclopedia game. That's the one other thing she got mad at —
RANDOLPH.   But it's a sure thing — *(From the path we see Miram Waslyk pushing her bike. Miriam is in her mid-thirties and wears a waitress uniform.)*
MIRIAM.   I'm home!
AMANDA.   Get out of here!
RANDOLPH.   No — *(He looks out the door as Miriam parks her bike.)* It's serious. She got her hair done.
AMANDA.   Please....
RANDOLPH.   Hi mom!
AMANDA.   *(Whispering sharply.)* I'm serious —
RANDOLPH.   Say you adore me —
AMANDA.   I adore you. Now go away —
RANDOLPH.   Say it in French.
AMANDA.   Je t'adore. Please Randolph ... *(He moves to the stairs.)*
RANDOLPH.   I think I'll take a nap. *(He climbs the stairs.)* Rest up for dinner.

AMANDA. You're not coming to — *(Miriam enters.)*
MIRIAM. Hi.
AMANDA. *(Thrown off.)* Hi.
MIRIAM. Well?
AMANDA. Well what? I'm just standing here.
MIRIAM. *(Referring to her hair.)* How do you like it?
AMANDA. *(Regaining poise.)* Nice. How much did it cost?
MIRIAM. Don't worry. I paid cash.
AMANDA. Somebody left more than a quarter tip today?
MIRIAM. I sold a painting. Hah. Whatta' ya think of that?
AMANDA. How much did you get for it?
MIRIAM. Whatever happened to "Congratulations Mom, nice job"?
AMANDA. Congratulations mom, nice job. How much?
MIRIAM. What's the difference — I spent it already.
AMANDA. Mother ...
MIRIAM. Nine dollars. *(Before Amanda can react.)* Don't start. I didn't even like it that much.
AMANDA. Which one was it?
MIRIAM. "Moon over the statue." *(Amanda looks blank.)* You know. That statue at the end of town. *(Amanda gets a calculator.)* The one where the plaque fell off and nobody can remember who he's supposed to be —
AMANDA. *(On the calculator.)* Let's see ... there's the paint ... and the brushes ...
MIRIAM. Cut it out —
AMANDA. Depreciation to pallet ... a canvas ... labor ...
MIRIAM. Don't count labor. I don't consider it labor.
AMANDA. Congratulations mother. You managed to lose approximately 23 dollars on that transaction.
MIRIAM. You look at it the wrong way Manda. Try this angle: this morning I had a painting that I really didn't like very much and this afternoon I have a haircut, that I desperately needed. *(Off Amanda's look.)* Well I did. I looked like a Pekinese. *(She plops down onto the couch.)* How was school?
AMANDA. Undemanding.
MIRIAM. Did Peter talk to you?
AMANDA. *(A sigh.)* Yes.

MIRIAM. Well? Did he ask you to the dance?

AMANDA. Yes.

MIRIAM. Great!

AMANDA. I told him I'd let him know.

MIRIAM. Why'd ya do that?

AMANDA. 'Cause I'm not sure —

MIRIAM. Call him up and say yes. I'll try and peddle a couple paintings and we'll buy you a new dress —

AMANDA. I don't need a new dress.

MIRIAM. *(Shaking her head.)* Sometimes I swear you're adopted. Go on, call him and say yes. The poor kid's probably suffering.

AMANDA. You don't even know him.

MIRIAM. Look kiddo, asking out a girl for a kid that age is a major traumatic experience. Asking you out in particular was an act of courage. *(Amanda says nothing.)* Go to the dance, Manda. You might have some fun.

AMANDA. They act like such kids.

MIRIAM. They are kids — they're allowed. Maybe you'll have a nice time with Peter. I thought you liked him.

AMANDA. He's okay. At least he doesn't wear t-shirts with rock groups on the front.

MIRIAM. So call.

AMANDA. I don't know ... he's shorter than I am.

MIRIAM. Give him a year.

AMANDA. And he has this pimple ...

MIRIAM. Lemmie give ya a tip, kiddo. You keep waitin' for perfection and you're gonna sit home a lot. Trust me.

AMANDA. Let me think about it, okay?

MIRIAM. Okay. *(Silence for a moment.)* The suspense is killing me. What'd you think of Warren?

AMANDA. He's all right. *(Amanda tries to avoid her. She absently thumbs through* Shogun.*)*

MIRIAM. I saw him down on the road. He said you had a nice talk.

AMANDA. Uh-huh.

MIRIAM. He also said you returned his watch. *(Amanda looks up from the book.)* Listen Manda, I want to explain about last night —

AMANDA. *(Very patronizing.)* You don't have to explain anything, mother.

MIRIAM. Would you please stop calling me "mother." I feel like Donna Reed when you do that.

AMANDA. What would you prefer?

MIRIAM. How about "mom"? It's short — very American. *(Off her look.)* Okay, how about "Miriam"? I don't mind. Call me Miriam.

AMANDA. *(Patiently.)* You are such a hippie sometimes. *(She rises.)* I have to finish the floor.

MIRIAM. No. Sit down a second please. *(She reluctantly does.)*

AMANDA. This is none of my business —

MIRIAM. Yes it is. Don't make it rough on me, okay? I'm trying to be an example here. Now, I've known Warren for a few years now —

AMANDA. He told me.

MIRIAM. Yeah, well, I wanted to make sure you knew that. I mean, I didn't want you to think your mother just goes out and picks up strange men. *(Amanda sighs.)* Please, save the patronizing sighs for later. This isn't easy. Now I've been feeling pretty dishonest all day. You know that I've had ... men stay here before, and I've always tried to be up front about it. I wasn't going to sneak around and live some lie just for appearances —

AMANDA. If I promise to call you Miriam can we drop all this?

MIRIAM. You should be grateful we can talk about things. I could never talk to my mother about anything. Especially sex.

AMANDA. She died when you were seven. How many chances did you have?

MIRIAM. Look ... last night ... I was out painting and Warren came by because ... well, he knew I was working on his birthday present ... and he sat on the blanket there and we talked while I painted — just like we used to do — and one thing led to another and ... you know ... then ... uhh ... this leads to that and ... ahh ... well, there you are. *(A beat.)*

AMANDA. I sure am glad we can talk about these things. *(She rises.)* Are we through?

MIRIAM. No. When you gave Warren back his watch it kind of ... embarrassed him, I guess. He really wants you to like him. I want you to like him. And you and I know we've had some problems in the past about this. But ... you're older now. And you-know-who is no longer with us. *(A devious laugh from upstairs.)* And between you and ... your friend, any man I brought home here didn't stand a chance.

AMANDA. *(Too innocent.)* What did I do?

MIRIAM. You intimidated the hell out of them, that's what —

AMANDA. If they're that insecure —

MIRIAM. Lemmie give ya a tip kiddo: men — on the whole — are scared to death of women.

AMANDA. Why?

MIRIAM. For one thing, we're smarter than they are. And they've got this thing about ... how they always have to be in charge — they have to have all the answers. And when they're confronted by a kid who has a 160 IQ — a kid who loves to show it off, I might add — then they get intimidated. And nothing runs faster than a man who feels intimidated — trust me. You'll learn this when you start dating. And then when you-know-who would show up —

AMANDA. I'm beyond that mother.

RANDOLPH. *(From upstairs.)* Hah!

MIRIAM. Well I'm glad of that. Because you're a strange enough kid without him around. *(The phone rings.)*

AMANDA and MIRIAM. Mrs. Simpers.

MIRIAM. Spare me.

AMANDA. *(Into phone.)* Hello Mrs. Simpers ... I just knew it was you ... no, the other offer still stands ...

MIRIAM. *(Whispering.)* What other offer?

AMANDA. It's not important who the other party is —

MIRIAM. *(Loudly.)* That's because there is no other party!

AMANDA. *(Hand over receiver.)* Will you stop it!

MIRIAM. Where'd you learn to lie like that? *(Miriam — in a good mood — decides to bust on Amanda, who manages to keep a*

34

straight face when on the phone.)
AMANDA. No ... but I'll tell you what I am willing to do —
MIRIAM. Oh please ... tell us — tell us ... *(She begins to tickle Amanda, who tries to move away.)*
AMANDA. Since you've been such a loyal customer in the past, all you have to do is match the other offer — *(Hand on receiver.)* Come on ... cut it out ... *(Into phone.)* That's right — still 1300 dollars ... *(She falls to the floor. Miriam keeps it up.)* Okay ... get back to me later. *(She hangs up and releases the laughter, scrambling away from her mother. They both sit on the floor, out of breath.)* What's the matter with you?
MIRIAM. I'm in a good mood.
AMANDA. I think she heard you —
MIRIAM. *(Picking up the quilt.)* Good. I don't wanta sell it to her Manda. She'll put it on display in the guest room. *(She twirls it around her like a cape.)* Quilts are meant to wrap up in.
AMANDA. Careful. You might pull a stitch.
MIRIAM. Don't insult me — this is quality workmanship. *(She tosses it over Amanda's head, covering her.)*
AMANDA. I like you better in a bad mood. *(She removes it and begins to fold it up.)*
MIRIAM. Whatta ya say — let's not sell it. *(Amanda simply shakes her head and keeps folding.)* I'm serious Manda. I don't think I wanta sell it. *(Amanda hands Miriam the quilt and moves to the desk.)* A painting I can knock out in a few days, but this ... this took a lot of time, picking the right colors ... mixing, matching ... textures ... *(She stands, holding onto it. Amanda crosses to her holding a ledger.)* It's sort of like giving birth. Better. It didn't destroy my hips. *(Amanda opens the ledger.)* Put that away.
AMANDA. This past January we were forced to buy a new furnace, remember?
MIRIAM. Yes.
AMANDA. And where did the down payment come from?
MIRIAM. The elves brought it. I forget.
AMANDA. *(Patiently.)* It came from the money we'd set aside to pay the school taxes, which are due at the end of the month — although 863 dollars a year to perpetuate that moron factory they call a school is a little ridiculous. Now, if I went

to a private school —

MIRIAM. Bag it kiddo. Even if we could afford it I wouldn't send ya to one of those. You're already a snob — I can imagine what they'd turn you into. *(Amanda begins to put the ledger away.)* Don't put that away yet. I need a check.

AMANDA. What for?

MIRIAM. I forgot to take one this morning. I still have to go back into town so we have something to eat tonight.

AMANDA. *(Nose in the ledger.)* Let me balance this first. *(A beat.)*

MIRIAM. You know we can get a 90 day extension on the taxes. *(Amanda looks up.)* I checked.

AMANDA. And what about my school trip? You said I could have ten percent to pay it off.

MIRIAM. Whatta' you wanta go to New York for anyway? It's big, it's dirty, it's noisy. Nobody speaks English.

AMANDA. Because I've never been there. I've never been anywhere.

MIRIAM. You are so deprived.

AMANDA. I want to see a Broadway show. I want to see museums. Anything besides this lousy town.

MIRIAM. Well ... Warren said he'd lend us the money. *(Amanda stares at her.)*

RANDOLPH. *(From upstairs.)* Still here if you need me.

MIRIAM. It would just be a loan. We'd pay it back.

AMANDA. Mother I am trying to comprehend this ... post partum depression you're having. But it's only a quilt. And we have to sell it. *(Hands Miriam a check.)* Don't make it out for more than twenty-seven dollars. *(She puts back the ledger and crosses for kitchen.)* I have to finish the floor. *(She exits. Miriam looks around the room, does a little half hearted straightening. She picks up Amanda's champagne glass and a few other things and heads back to dining room table.)*

MIRIAM. I think we'll eat by candlelight. It'll hide some of the dirt. *(She goes to put the glass on the table when something catches her eye: the other champagne glass. She thinks a moment, then sips from the first glass, puts it down, picks up the other one and repeats the process. She holds them both for a moment, then puts them back on the table.)* Amanda! *(Amanda enters from kitchen.)*

AMANDA. What?

MIRIAM. *(Containing her anger.)* How old are you? *(A beat.)*

AMANDA. Is this a trick question?

MIRIAM. How old?

AMANDA. Mother —

MIRIAM. Answer the question! *(Randolph appears on the stairs.)*

RANDOLPH. She knows I'm here ...

AMANDA. Thirteen. *(Randolph moves in on Miriam, observing.)*

MIRIAM. Thirteen. Now, when you were four, I thought it was cute. When you were seven and you took him to school with you, I got a little worried. When you were nine, I thought it might be time for psychiatric help — but then he disappeared. About the same time Morty did. And now — lo and behold — Randolph is back ... goddamnit!

AMANDA. How'd you know?

MIRIAM. I know everything — I'm your mother!

RANDOLPH. Someone must've told her —

MIRIAM. *(Observing Amanda.)* He's here now, isn't he?

RANDOLPH. Someone in black knee socks —

MIRIAM. Where? Where is he? *(She swings her arms around, narrowly missing Randolph, who feints and shadow boxes back.)*

RANDOLPH. She is seriously disturbed —

MIRIAM. What do I have to do? What? Call in an exorcist? Rub garlic on the windows — what?

AMANDA. *(Not as confident.)* That's ridiculous —

MIRIAM. No more ridiculous than a thirteen year old girl with an imaginary friend!

RANDOLPH. I don't have to take this. *(He turns and disappears upstairs.)*

MIRIAM. What is your problem? Why is it the minute I show some interest in someone besides you that this happens?

AMANDA. Well what do we need Warren around for anyway?

MIRIAM. We don't need him kiddo — I do! *(Amanda says nothing. Miriam takes a deep breath, calming.)* It's not always just gonna be you and me, Manda. Things change. And you're not gonna want to spend your Saturday nights goin' to the movies with me or ... or sittin' on the side of a mountain while I paint. And I know when it comes time for college you'll

37

pick one a thousand miles from here — you've made that plain enough. Where's that leave me kiddo?

AMANDA. *(Quietly.)* You don't have to stay here.

MIRIAM. I like it here. And I'd like somebody to be with — I don't think that's askin' a lot. I'm not sayin' I'm gonna run off and marry him, I just want ... I don't wanta be alone all the time, can't you understand that?

AMANDA. Why him?

MIRIAM. What difference does it make? I could bring home Albert Einstein and you'd make fun of his hair. I know Warren doesn't meet your standards but he's ... he's ... a nice man. I like him. And all I'm asking for is a nice quiet dinner. *(Advancing on Amanda.)* A nice quiet dinner. Because at the first sign of any uninvited guests the trip to New York is cancelled. *(She turns and crosses to the yard. Amanda follows her.)*

AMANDA. You promised! That's not fair —

MIRIAM. I gave birth to you; I don't have to be fair.

AMANDA. Fine. You want me to be civil to the mailman, fine.

MIRIAM. He has a name.

AMANDA. Should I call him Uncle Warren like I did with the others. Uncle Steve, Uncle Morty ...

MIRIAM. Why? You wanta' answer me that — why do you do this?

AMANDA. He'll change everything —

MIRIAM. How do you know? You never give anyone a chance, you never ... damnit, I wish once in your life you'd think about somebody else! *(She picks up her bike.)* A nice quiet dinner, understand? Or I'm taking out a second mortgage and you are seeing a psychiatrist because there is something very wrong here! *(She starts to push her bike off stage — stops.)* I am going to say something now that I swore I would *never* say to any child of mine. *(A beat. She smiles coldly.)* I can't wait till you have a daughter. *(She exits. Amanda stands a moment, then sits on the porch steps. Randolph appears at the top of the stairs and speaks as he crosses outside.)*

RANDOLPH. *(Imitating Amanda.)* I trust him Randolph. Mother won't find out. *(Amanda says nothing.)* Warren wouldn't tell ... I trust him.

AMANDA.   Get it over with.

RANDOLPH.   Told ya so — told ya so ...

AMANDA.   I can't believe he did that.

RANDOLPH.   He did. *(He takes out a cigarette and puts it into his holder.)* He squealed ... ratted ... finked ... "dropped a dime"... *(He sits next to her.)* Warren Zimmerman is a tattle tale. *(Silence for a moment.)* I'm starved.

AMANDA.   You can't be. You're a figment of my imagination.

RANDOLPH.   Get yourself something to eat then.   I'm famished. *(Silence.)*

AMANDA.   Wonder what's for dinner.

RANDOLPH.   *(Smiling.)* Mailman. *(He lights his cigarette.)*

THE LIGHTS FADE

END ACT ONE

ACT TWO

SCENE 1

As the houselights fade, we hear the beginning of Mozart's Horn Concerto #3. As stage lights rise the music switches from house speakers to a a small tape player on the table. The lights rise and we see Miriam, Warren and Amanda all seated on the floor eating dinner with chopsticks. Warren and Miriam drink wine. There is a wok in the middle of the floor. Except for the music there is absolute silence. It seems a little tense. Randolph appears at the top of the stairs. He now wears the outfit of a seafaring man from an earlier century and has grown a mustache since the first act. He surveys the scene below.

RANDOLPH. Well ... isn't this a nice, quiet dinner. *(Amanda ignores him; he comes down the stairs and makes himself comfortable. The silence continues until finally ...)*

WARREN. This is very good.

MIRIAM. Thank you.

RANDOLPH. *(Observing.)* He does chew with his mouth closed — I'll give him that much.

MIRIAM. *(Picking up the wok.)* Finish it up.

WARREN. No. No thanks. Full. *(Silence.)* Everything was really good. *(He directs this at Amanda. She nods. Silence.)* I haven't had goulash in years. *(Silence. Miriam and Warren exchange a look.)* Your mom tells me you started *Shogun.*

AMANDA. *(A shrug.)* First ninety pages.

RANDOLPH. I don't like this book. These boots are bloody uncomfortable.

WARREN. Ninety pages?

AMANDA. I had some time before dinner.

RANDOLPH. Read some Hemingway. I need a tan.

WARREN. How do you like it?

RANDOLPH. *(Leaning into Warren.)* It's better than when she

40

read *Little Women.*

AMANDA. It's okay.

RANDOLPH. It does have its good points ... *(He pulls a dagger from his sash.)* Let me show you how we deal with tattletales ... *(He moves behind Warren, holding up the dagger.)*

WARREN. Are you interested in the Orient?

AMANDA. *(At Randolph.)* No! *(Warren is a little shocked at her tone of voice. Miriam shoots her a look and then, suspecting Randolph is in the room, glances around looking for him. She stops, realizing how ridiculous she must look. Warren observes both of them; Randolph smiles and puts away his dagger.)*

WARREN. Well, uhhh ... I thought you might be, with the chopsticks and everything. *(The phone rings.)*

MIRIAM. *(Still glaring at Amanda.)* We always use them.

AMANDA. They're easy to wash. *(Into phone.)* Hello Mrs. Simpers ... I just knew it was you ... I see ... *(Off.)* We've got her where we want her. Should I finalize?

MIRIAM. You do what you want.

AMANDA. Could you give me a definite answer please? *(Vaguely.)* I mean ... after what you were ... you know ... this afternoon ...

WARREN. Should I step outside?

MIRIAM. No. *(To Amanda.)* Do what you want.

AMANDA. *(A sigh.)* I can't talk right now Mrs. Simpers — could you call me back later ... thank you. *(She hangs up and glares at her mother. Miriam glares back. Warren just sort of looks back and forth.)*

MIRIAM. Why don't you clear the floor and make some coffee? *(Amanda rises, picking up plates.)*

AMANDA. Should I leave the music on?

WARREN. Please do. I love the horn concertos. *(This stops her.)*

RANDOLPH. I'll bet.

WARREN. I'm not too good at telling them apart though. I know it was E-flat major — but is that two or three? They're very similar, I get confused. *(A beat. Amanda stares at him.)*

RANDOLPH. He's showing off.

AMANDA. Three. It was number three.

WARREN. Thanks.

AMANDA. *(Still staring.)* You're welcome. *(She crosses to the kitchen. Randolph follows.)*

RANDOLPH. Don't act so impressed. He probably looked at the label. *(They exit.)*

MIRIAM. I had no idea you were a classical music fan.

WARREN. *(Whispering.)* I looked at the label. Did she really read 90 pages before dinner?

MIRIAM. She's a speed reader.

WARREN. Oh.

MIRIAM. *(Filling their wine glasses.)* Last year on her birthday I gave her a stereo. A really nice stereo. Saved for eight months. And she took one look at it and I knew something was wrong, and she said it was very nice but what she had really wanted was a speed reading course. So, I got the money back on the stereo and she went to Evelyn Wood.

WARREN. Most mothers would be thrilled by something like that.

MIRIAM. Yeah, I guess. *(Shaking her head.)* Boy, I really wanted that stereo. *(She refills their glasses.)* She's always been that way. When she was four I gave her all my old Barbie dolls and she asked what she was supposed to do with them. *(Putting back the bottle.)* Actually, I was kind of glad. I think Barbie dolls have done more to screw up women in this country than anything else, I really do. We all expected to grow up and be built like that. *(Amanda re-enters carrying a pie tin full of scraps.)*

AMANDA. Your turn or mine?

MIRIAM. *(Taking the tin.)* Mine. I want Warren to meet him. *(Amanda crosses back to kitchen as Miriam heads outside.)* C'mon.

WARREN. *(Following her outside.)* Who are we meeting?

MIRIAM. Our pet raccoon. *(She climbs over the fence and moves upstage.)* For years he raided our garbage cans, so we came to sort of a truce. Works out fine: our garbage cans are spared and Amanda got the pet she always wanted. *(Calling off stage.)* Here Morty! C'mere boy ... *(Turning back to Warren.)* She named him. *(He helps as she climbs back over. They stand against the fence a moment; Warren holds onto her hand a moment, then lets go. Silence.)*

42

WARREN. So ... how was your day? *(She shrugs.)* Could it be my imagination ... or were you kind of ... avoiding me at lunch?

MIRIAM. Course not.

WARREN. Miriam ...

MIRIAM. All right, maybe a little.

WARREN. Why?

MIRIAM. I don't know. Thought maybe we'd ... I don't know — use up all our conversation and have nothing to talk about at dinner.

WARREN. We didn't talk at dinner. We just sort of ... chewed. And glared at each other.

MIRIAM. Yeah, well I'm sorry it turned out that way.

WARREN. I started a big fight, huh?

MIRIAM. It's not your fault.

WARREN. She was really very nice to me today. Most of the time.

MIRIAM. Oh, she is nice. Most of the time. As her mother of course I'm prejudiced. I'm contractually obligated to love her. But ... I mean, she can be fun ... in a ... Republican sort of way.

WARREN. That's what was so weird. One minute she was perfectly polite and the next minute she was ... Bette Davis.

MIRIAM. Yeah, well ... she has a little help with that. Her friend Randolph was here today. You — of course — didn't see him because he's invisible. *(He says nothing, simply staring at her.)* Should I finish the story or have you heard enough to sufficiently scare you off?

WARREN. Takes more than that.

MIRIAM. Randolph's her imaginary friend. *(Before he can react.)* I know — she's too old for that sort of thing. And — typical Amanda — she had to invent someone who's perfect. I mean, most kids make up talking animals or something. Not her. She had to conjure up James Bond. *(Observing him.)* This is where most men find an excuse to leave. They figure they'll wake up some night and Amanda will be looming over them with an axe. *(Looking off.)* There he is. Evening Morty! *(Warren looks.)* Well fed, huh?

WARREN. I've never seen a raccoon that ... lumbered before.

MIRIAM. We take good care of him. She wanted a dog but ... *(A shrug.)* This was cheaper. *(She moves away.)* I don't know, Warren. I get angry at her and at the same time I can't entirely blame her. I grew up in this house, but back then there were ... people around. For most of her life it's just been the two of us up here. And she's always been a misfit at school — partly by choice. I even enrolled her in Sunday School one time to try and find some friends for her. Lasted one week. She's the only kid ever got bounced from Sunday School. Kept asking the teacher how the ark managed to stay afloat if Noah had brought on two termites.

WARREN. Not a bad question when you think about it.

MIRIAM. Yeah, well it was probably Randolph's. He's always the instigator — especially when there's a man around. It was Randolph who invented the Encyclopedia Game — and that managed to intimidate any guy who came within a mile of the place.

WARREN. What's the Encyclopedia Game?

MIRIAM. Don't ask and don't worry. She's been warned — you won't be subjected to it.

WARREN. Let her.

MIRIAM. No.

WARREN. I'm serious.

MIRIAM. So am I. No.

WARREN. Why not?

MIRIAM. Because I said so.

WARREN. You can't force her to like me, Miriam. Look at it from her point of view. Before she even meets me, she finds out I spent the night. Not exactly a great first impression for a kid. And it's my fault; I forgot the watch.

MIRIAM. It wasn't just that. I could tell by the way she acted this morning. She probably heard us.

WARREN. *(Embarrassed.)* Oh no ...

MIRIAM. I don't mean she heard *that*, I mean ... *(She glances around.)* Can I ask you a personal question?

WARREN. Sure.

MIRIAM. After you ... make love ... do you always laugh like that?

44

WARREN. Well, I don't smoke. *(She looks at him a second, then laughs.)* I laugh when I'm nervous or relaxed and at that point in time I was ... relaxed. Very relaxed. *(He begins to laugh.)* Incredibly relaxed. *(He stops laughing.)* Too relaxed. I fell asleep, didn't I?

MIRIAM. *(A shrug.)* You're a man.

WARREN. I got so mad at myself today when I thought about it. I didn't want to fall asleep first.

MIRIAM. It was late —

WARREN. I wanted to watch you sleep. I wanted to see if it was how I'd pictured it.

MIRIAM. *(Wary.)* How had you pictured it? I hope it wasn't with my mouth open or anything.

WARREN. Oh, I've pictured you lots of ways. You probably noticed last night that I'm a pretty sound sleeper. You can put halfa' sticka' dynamite right in the bed with me — I'm not wakin' up. Well, that's a recently acquired talent. *(He sits on the fence rail.)* I'd been a terrible sleeper since I was a kid. And then I got out of the service and ... my marriage broke up, and it got even worse. And then — and I feel really stupid saying this — but my whole life was changed by Reader's Digest. I don't subscribe or anything. I was at the dentist's. So I read this article about sleep problems and I realized that all these years, I had been picking bedtime to worry about things. And the article said to think about pleasant things — what a revelation, huh? *(He laughs.)*

MIRIAM. Was that nervous or relaxed?

WARREN. Relaxed. Mostly. Eighty-five percent. *(He laughs again.)* Think pleasant things — it's so simple — and all those years ... *(He shrugs.)* Anyway, I started to think about you. *(He hops off the fence, crossing to her.)* You would not believe some of the places we've been together. I'm talking two full passports. And you should see the presents you've gotten. Miriam, you are the best dressed woman in this town. *(He catches himself. Points to his head.)* Up here.

MIRIAM. You really do that?

WARREN. Couple years now. Five, six nights a week.

MIRIAM. What do you think about on the other nights?

WARREN. Fishing. I don't want you to get spoiled.

MIRIAM. I don't get it Warren. Why did you wait all this time for me to invite you out?

WARREN. I was afraid of screwing up what I already had.

MIRIAM. Which was?

WARREN. Lunch. Come on, tell the truth. Have you ever seen anyone who enjoys his lunch as much as I do? *(She shakes her head.)* And if I had asked you out and you'd said no then — well ... things might've changed. You might've felt awkward ... avoided me — like you did today ... or something — who knows. And, I felt funny because I'm older —

MIRIAM. Not that much —

WARREN. I didn't want to chance it. I had forty-five great minutes a day with a woman. There's a lotta married guys can't say that. And then today when you were ... ya know, kind of ... ignoring me ... well, I got a little scared.

MIRIAM. What about?

WARREN. Losing my lunch. *(He realizes.)* Oh God, that sounded awful. I don't mean it like that I just ... well, not that I'm that experienced with these things but when you spend the night with someone you either get ... involved or you don't. But ... ya never seem to go back to just bein' friends. *(Silence.)*

MIRIAM. *(Shivering.)* Gettin' colder.

WARREN. Supposed to rain tonight.

MIRIAM. Really? *(He nods.)* Hope it holds off. Have to finish your present.

WARREN. It can wait.

MIRIAM. *(Shaking her head.)* Nope. Have to catch the moon *tonight* at the right time. Otherwise it ... *(Catching herself.)* That's just the way it is. It sounds goofy —

WARREN. You're an artist.

MIRIAM. *(Smiling.)* I love having that for an excuse. You can get away with almost anything if people think you're an artist. *(Silence. Then, they both try and speak at the same time.)* Go ahead.

WARREN. No, you.

MIRIAM. I was just gonna say ... we can use the rain. What were you gonna say?

WARREN. I love you. *(She is unsure how to react.)*
MIRIAM. *(Shaking her head.)* No ...
WARREN. *(Unsure.)* What?
MIRIAM. Just no ... don't ...
WARREN. Why not?
MIRIAM. Just don't — that's all.
WARREN. I wanted to say that to you last night. Wanted to say it about a hundred times. I just ... just didn't want you to think I was saying it to get you into bed.
MIRIAM. *(Gently.)* Warren, you didn't get me into bed. I got you into bed.
WARREN. Well, yeah. But next time it's my idea, okay? *(He takes a ring box from his pocket.)* This is just a little something for taking the initiative. *(He hands it to her. She holds it — wary.)*
MIRIAM. What is this?
WARREN. Shoes. I wasn't sure of the size, I think they're gonna be small —
MIRIAM. *(Moving away.)* Cut it out Warren.
WARREN. Open it. *(She doesn't.)* I know, I know ... I must look incredibly pushy —
MIRIAM. Little bit, yeah —
WARREN. I don't want an answer tonight. *(A nervous laugh.)* Who'm I kiddin'? I would love an answer tonight. I just ... understand if I don't get one ... *(She moves away, looking up at the house.)*
MIRIAM. It's just that it's very complicated —
WARREN. Why?
MIRIAM. Because I still have to get my daughter's approval.
WARREN. *(Smiling.)* Besides that —
MIRIAM. I'm serious.
WARREN. You're a grown woman Miriam —
MIRIAM. And she's my daughter. *(Touching him.)* I'm sorry ... believe me, I'm sorry, but I have to think of her too. So we have to ... see how things go. *(Silence.)*
WARREN. Okay. *(He holds out the box.)* Least take a look at it.
MIRIAM. No.
WARREN. Go ahead.
MIRIAM. *(Slightly irritated.)* Warren, don't push, okay — *(He*

47

puts it into her hands.)

WARREN. I've got the receipt. It's okay if you don't like it. I'm not real experienced at pickin' this stuff out —

MIRIAM. I'll love it. That's the problem. *(She looks at the box.)* I did have a diamond ring once. For 19 months. My mother's engagement ring — my father gave it to me right before he died. It was ... ornate to say the least. Not exactly fashionable but ... I tend to prefer things like that. *(Shrugs.)* But ... first time on my own ... things come up you don't expect. Manda was maybe three and she needed ... you know — things add up. *(Nodding towards the house.)* Shame the kid wasn't older. She would've gotten me a much better price I'm sure. *(She hands it back to him.)*

WARREN. If it makes you feel any better you're not the first bride without a diamond. Jeannie and I got married kind of quick because of me gettin' drafted and we couldn't afford a diamond and a wedding. *(Miriam gives him questioning look. He attempts to lighten things up.)* This town gets real suspicious when you have a rushed wedding. Had a little reception down the Elks, and people would say, "Hey! Congratulations, when ya due?"

MIRIAM. *(Quietly.)* You don't know, do you?

WARREN. *(Stumped.)* Probably not. What're we talking about?

MIRIAM. I've never been married. *(A beat.)*

WARREN. You were never married?

MIRIAM. Nope. *(He glances up at the house.)* That's right. She's a little bastard.

WARREN. I didn't mean to ... it's just you never said anything so I assumed maybe it was an ugly divorce or something so I never asked.

MIRIAM. I can't believe you didn't know this. My God, fourteen years ago I was the biggest topic of conversation in this town.

WARREN. I wasn't around fourteen years ago.

MIRIAM. Well ... now ya know.

WARREN. Does her father ever visit?

MIRIAM. Her father ... *(Shakes her head, laughing.)* Her father was my art history professor and he was perfect. I was very much into perfection back then. He was a genius, a snob, smoked a pipe, called people "facists" if they disagreed with him — that was very "in" back then ... even his name was perfect: Frederik, with a "K". Isn't that a perfect name for a pipe smoking artist — Frederik with a "K"?

WARREN. If you don't mind having it misspelled all the time ...

MIRIAM. *(Not really hearing him.)* And when I went to him and told him I was pregnant he was quite calm and said we'd discuss it when he got back from Europe. I never saw him again. For all I know he's teaching at Oxford.

WARREN. She's never met her father?

MIRIAM. No, but she's managed to pick up a lot of his traits. My daughter is the classic example of genetics over environment. At first I was quite angry ... naturally. But what's the point? I'll say this for Frederik: he got me off my search-for-perfection kick.

WARREN. Hey, if you're lookin' for imperfection, I'm the guy for you. *(She laughs.)* I've got flaws you wouldn't believe.

MIRIAM. Like what?

WARREN. Like the way I just proposed. I assumed this was a second marriage for both of us and I ... toss you a ring. *(Amanda and Randolph emerge from the kitchen. Amanda carries tray with coffee.)* This is your first time, I've gotta do this right. *(He leads her to the steps and gets down on one knee as Randolph and Amanda reach the front door.)*

RANDOLPH. You better hope he's doing a Jolson impression ...

AMANDA. Coffee's ready. *(Miriam stands quickly, attempting to hide the ring box.)* Inside or out?

MIRIAM. We'll be in in a minute. *(Amanda and Randolph head back into living room.)*

RANDOLPH. Did you happen to notice what she had in her hand?

AMANDA. Shhh ...

MIRIAM. *(Handing him the box.)* We'll talk about this later, okay?

WARREN. You can hold onto it —

MIRIAM. No. *(She climbs the fence to retrieve Morty's plate.)*

RANDOLPH. Do you realize what she becomes if she marries him? Miriam Zimmerman. I can see it now: "Season's Greetings from Warren and Miriam Zimmerman." You may lose a mother but you'll gain a tongue twister. *(Amanda turns to say something to him as Miriam and Warren enter.)*

MIRIAM. What time is it?

AMANDA. Quarter to nine. What time's your moon?

MIRIAM. Little while. *(Amanda climbs the stairs; Randolph does not.)*

RANDOLPH. Where are you going?

MIRIAM. Where ya goin'?

AMANDA. *(Aimed at both of them.)* Upstairs.

RANDOLPH. Get back here.

MIRIAM. Don't you want some cake?

AMANDA. Maybe later.

RANDOLPH. He's proposing. It's kamikaze time —

WARREN. Come on, don't go yet. It's my birthday party. Maybe we'll play a game or something. *(Amanda stops. Miriam glares at Warren.)*

RANDOLPH. Ahhh ... an opening. Go for it.

AMANDA. I don't know any games.

RANDOLPH. *(To Warren.)* Yes she does —

WARREN. What about the Encyclopedia Game?

RANDOLPH. I think I'm starting to like him.

WARREN. Your mom told me about it.

AMANDA. *(Glancing at her mother.)* It's dumb.

MIRIAM. She's right.

WARREN. Let me decide. Come on ... your mom won't mind. *(Turning to Miriam.)* Will you? *(Miriam glares at Warren, then at Amanda.)*

MIRIAM. Go ahead if you want.

AMANDA. Be right back. *(Randolph follows her upstairs.)*

RANDOLPH. It's a trick. They're in this together ... *(They exit.)*

MIRIAM. What're you doing?

WARREN. She wants to play it; you forbid it. That gives her another reason to hate me.

MIRIAM.   You're undermining my authority —

WARREN.   She's thirteen. Your authority gets undermined every time she leaves the house —

MIRIAM.   I don't like it —

WARREN.   Let her take her best shot. Get it out of her system.

MIRIAM.   You don't understand, Warren. She's memorizing the encyclopedia.

WARREN.   World Book or Britannica?

MIRIAM.   It's cruel. She wants to make you look stupid ... to embarrass you so you'll go away ...

WARREN.   I don't mind.

MIRIAM.   I do —

WARREN.   *(Holding out box.)* You sure you don't want to at least look at this?

MIRIAM.   I don't believe you just did that. I'm trying to make things as easy as possible on you —

WARREN.   You're makin' this sound like an audition —

MIRIAM.   You know what I mean —

WARREN.   What if she doesn't give me the part?

MIRIAM.   *(Moving away from him.)* She's like her father when she does these things. Nobody on my side of the family ever acted like this. *(He looks a the ring box a moment, then puts it back into his pocket.)*

WARREN.   Is Randolph here now?

MIRIAM.   He will be once the game starts.

WARREN.   Good. *(Amanda and Randolph enter from upstairs. She carries four volumes of encyclopedia.)*

RANDOLPH.   Whatever you do, don't lay the "I'm just a kid bit" on too thick. I hate that part.

WARREN.   You're not bringing the whole thing down are you?

AMANDA.   We'll use volumes A to E and and the first 98 pages of F. *(During the course of this scene, Miriam gathers her painting equipment and puts it by the front door.)* Now, it's really pretty simple. You use one of the books, and you can ask me any question — except for like populations and elevations —

WARREN.   Why not them?

AMANDA.   Because they change.

WARREN. Elevations change?

AMANDA. You know what I mean. Then I ask you a question and we get a point for each one we get right. We usually play to 21.

WARREN. Sounds good. What's the point spread? *(She glances at Randolph. Warren follows her glance, which he will do for the remainder of the scene.)*

AMANDA. I beg your pardon?

WARREN. Don't you think I deserve some sort of handicap?

RANDOLPH. Ohhh ... I could say something tasteless now.

WARREN. You're in shape for this. I haven't even looked at an encyclopedia since I did a report on Rutherford B. Hayes —

AMANDA. *(Immediately.)* Nineteenth president.

WARREN. Eighteenth.

AMANDA. *(Embarrassed.)* Well, I didn't get to "H" yet.

WARREN. *(Heading for the stairs.)* That's what I mean; you've been in training. Plus, you've got the home court advantage. *(He starts up the stairs.)* But don't worry, I think I've got an idea that'll even it all out.

RANDOLPH. Where's he going?

AMANDA. Where're you going?

WARREN. To the bathroom. Don't worry, I remember the way. *(He starts up, stops.)* Oh, ahh ... you were right a minute ago. Hayes was the nineteenth president. It's an old poker trick ... checkin' the other guy's confidence. *(He winks and exits up the stairs.)*

RANDOLPH. Ohhh ... now he really gets it. *(Amanda turns to Miriam, who turns away.)*

AMANDA. It's his idea.

MIRIAM. Don't worry Amanda. I've grown to accept the fact that nothing is ever your fault. *(She goes about gathering her things.)*

RANDOLPH. Ask her about that ring. *(She shakes her head. Miriam notices.)*

MIRIAM. Oh, sorry Randolph. Forgot you were here. How've you been? *(To Amanda.)* Think the IRS would let me deduct him next year? It'd be a good deal — he doesn't eat much. Look into that for me, will you?

RANDOLPH.   *(Leaning into Miriam's face.)* Are you going to marry him?

AMANDA.   You gonna marry him?

MIRIAM.   *(Surprised.)* He asked me.

AMANDA.   What'd you say?

MIRIAM.   I said I didn't know.

AMANDA.   *(Smiling slightly.)* Oh ... okay.

MIRIAM.   And I hope that makes you happy. Both of you. *(She heads for the kitchen.)*

AMANDA.   Mother —

MIRIAM.   *(Cold.)* Just play your cruel little game and get it over with, okay? *(She exits into the kitchen. Silence for a moment, then Amanda turns to Randolph.)*

AMANDA.   *(Whispering.)* Well, now you did it. She's really mad.

RANDOLPH.   I did it?

AMANDA.   Just keep quiet will you! You're getting me confused —

RANDOLPH.   *(Loudly.)* You're confused?

AMANDA.   Shhhh!

RANDOLPH.   I'm the one who's confused! You call me to come help you and all I've been getting is abuse —

AMANDA.   Will you stop it —

RANDOLPH.   I will not stop it! You've been unpleasant all day. And if that's not enough ... *(He points accusingly at the copy of Shogun.)* Do you have any idea what happens in the next couple of pages? I know you do — you glanced ahead. I get thrown into a pit! A pit! Do you have any idea what that's going to do to my clothes? *(Unnoticed, Warren enters on the stairs.)*

AMANDA.   *(To Randolph.)* Are you finished?

WARREN.   Yeah. *(Amanda and Randolph both jump.)* Why? I take too long? *(Amanda shakes her head as he comes down.)* Okay ... ready for my proposition to even things out? *(Miriam enters from the kitchen, drying some paint brushes.)*

AMANDA.   Do you really think that's necessary? Maybe I've read a little more, but you've got all that life experience on me. After all Warren, I'm just a kid. *(Randolph and Miriam make a gagging motion. Amanda shoots Randolph a "knock it off" look.*

Warren follows where Amanda looks.)

WARREN. Something bothering you?

RANDOLPH. *(Leaning into him.)* Yes: you.

AMANDA. No.

WARREN. It's just that you keep ... *(Again, he observes her gaze.)* Well, glancing away. *(He suddenly flails one arm out in Randolph's direction, letting out a yell. Everyone jumps, including Randolph.)* Sorry. Muscle spasm. *(Randolph staggers away, clutching his chest.)*

RANDOLPH. He's one of those deranged veterans. *(Again, he follows Amanda's glance. Warren moves around to where Randolph stands and backs him up against the wall.)*

WARREN. Now, you do have a definite advantage —

RANDOLPH. It's called a brain —

WARREN. Which is why I'd like to propose a rule change.

AMANDA. What kind of change? *(He suddenly stamps his foot down, causing Randolph to leap up and move away. Warren points to the floor.)*

WARREN. Bug. *(He turns and crosses away.)* I brought along a book of my own. *(Picks up a photo album from under his coat.)*

RANDOLPH. I told you — totally deranged!

WARREN. My clients. Volume I. Now, here's my idea. For every question I ask you from the encyclopedia, I get to ask you one out of my book.

AMANDA. There's no logic to that Warren. They're just pictures.

WARREN. Of people. People who live in this town.

AMANDA. *(Tapping her volume.)* These are facts —

WARREN. And facts are fine, but you don't sit next to them on the bus everyday. You have to live with people. *(He glances around the room. Randolph flinches.)* Real, live people.

RANDOLPH. What's that supposed to mean?

AMANDA. How do I know you won't make something up?

MIRIAM. Amanda —

WARREN. I won't. Trust me.

RANDOLPH. Trust you? *(Into his face.)* Ha—ha—ha!

WARREN. Only a game. Right?

AMANDA. I suppose.

RANDOLPH. Don't put any money on it.

WARREN. So, I ask you one — you ask me one, then I ask one from my book. That'll be my handicap.

AMANDA. Choose your volume.

WARREN. I think I'll start with "A".

RANDOLPH. How original. (*Warren looks through the volume. Amanda is impatient to start.*)

AMANDA. Go ahead. (*Warren keeps looking.*) Ask me anything. (*Still looking.*) Anything you want ... anything at all ...

WARREN. Okay. (*She gets ready.*) What is ... Alabama? (*Amanda simply stares at him. Miriam, on the other side of the room, lets out a small laugh, then stifles it.*)

AMANDA. Excuse me?

WARREN. What is Alabama?

AMANDA. Look, if you're not going to take this seriously —

WARREN. I am —

AMANDA. Then why don't you ask me what the official flower is? The Camellia. How about the official bird: the Yellowhammer. Motto? *Audemus jura nostra defendre:* we dare defend our rights! (*She sits back, smiling smugly.*)

WARREN. You still haven't answered the question.

AMANDA. It's a stupid question —

WARREN. Not if you live there.

AMANDA. (*Frustrated.*) It's a state! Okay? Happy? It's a state.

WARREN. Very good. One point. Your turn. (*He hands her the volume.*)

MIRIAM. I've got to get going soon. I'll put dessert out — you can help yourselves. (*She enters kitchen.*)

RANDOLPH. (*Hanging over her shoulder.*) Humiliate him ...

AMANDA. What is the primary ingredient used to make up acrylics?

WARREN. (*Immediately.*) Got me.

AMANDA. Guess.

WARREN. No idea. My turn.

AMANDA. Give you a hint. It's a liquid.

WARREN. Water.

AMANDA. Be logical Warren. You can't make anything from just water.

WARREN. Ice.

AMANDA. Petroleum! The main ingredient in acrylics is petroleum. *(She and Randolph observe him, waiting for a response.)*
WARREN. *(Calmly.)* Sonuvagun.
RANDOLPH. He has a high tolerance for humiliation.
WARREN. *(Moving to wine.)* Let me get a fresh glass of wine, then it's my turn.
AMANDA. May I ask you a question?
WARREN. Sure.
AMANDA. Do you have to go to college to be a mailman?
WARREN. No.
RANDOLPH. Course not. It's a government job. *(Amanda stifles a laugh. Warren follows her gaze.)*
WARREN. Well, let me get my book. *(He moves to get it and stumbles slightly, tossing his wine all over Randolph.)*
RANDOLPH. Look what he did! Look!
WARREN. Geeez, I'm sorry.
AMANDA. Don't worry about it —
RANDOLPH. Look at this! I'm stained! I hate that!
WARREN. Could you get me a sponge, I'll clean this up.
AMANDA. *(Her attention divided.)* That rug is a sponge Warren. Don't worry about it.
RANDOLPH. *(Looking at his shirt.)* God, I hate that!
WARREN. You're sure?
AMANDA. I'm sure. We spill things all the time. Mother says it gives the rug character.
RANDOLPH. Get back to the game! I want this man humiliated!
WARREN. Okay, if you say so.
RANDOLPH. I want him out of here!
WARREN. *(Holding his album.)* Ready? *(He hands her the album.)*
RANDOLPH. Did you hear me? I want him out of here now!
WARREN. There's about 20 — 25 pictures in there. I want you to find the person who was in *Gone With the Wind.*
AMANDA. Somebody from here was in *Gone With the Wind?* *(He nods. She starts to open the book — stops.)*
RANDOLPH. That does it. You're on your own. *(He sits, defiantly, pouting.)*
AMANDA. How'm I supposed to do this?

56

WARREN. Observe. You can tell a lot about a person by just observing.
AMANDA. Was it a big role?
WARREN. No.
AMANDA. *(Pointing.)* Her?
WARREN. Interesting choice.
AMANDA. Is it right? Do I get a point?
WARREN. Hold on a second. What is it that you ... observed that makes you think it's her? *(Amanda and Randolph both sigh.)*
AMANDA. She's the right age —
WARREN. Good.
AMANDA. And she ... I don't know. She's just ... really pretty.
RANDOLPH. For an old person.
AMANDA. Am I right?
WARREN. Nope.
AMANDA. It's a stupid game.
WARREN. You really don't know who that is?
AMANDA. Why should I?
WARREN. She calls you all the time. *(Amanda is blank.)* Always five rings.
AMANDA. That's her? *(Warren nods.)* It doesn't look like her.
WARREN. You've never seen her —
AMANDA. You know what I mean. She looks ... so nice.
WARREN. What'd she ever do to you that was so terrible?
AMANDA. Well, nothing to me —
WARREN. Do you know anybody who knows her?
AMANDA. No, but —
WARREN. But everybody hates her, right?
RANDOLPH. It's a tradition —
WARREN. Because nobody knows her. She is ... well, incredibly shy. Took me three months of waving up to her window before she spoke to me — then it took another month before she came downstairs and opened the door. Little ... peculiar. She actually opens junk mail. Really, she writes back to all of them. Sometimes when I had extra I'd give it to her. That's a federal offense, by the way, so don't tell anybody. *(Handing back the book.)* Consider that a practice round. Try again.
AMANDA. I give up. This is stupid.

WARREN. *(Pointing to picture.)* Recognize him?

AMANDA. No.

WARREN. Look closer. *(She does.)*

AMANDA. It looks like ... the crossing guard.

WARREN. His name is Harry Pugh and he's been in hundreds of movies. And you pass by him everyday and didn't even know it.

AMANDA. Who was he in *Gone With the Wind?*

WARREN. Well, you know that scene at the hospital where the soldier has to have his leg amputated —

AMANDA. That was him?

WARREN. Not quite. After that, when Scarlett leaves, and the camera pulls back and you see all those Confederate soldiers? *(She nods.)* He's one of them. Viven Leigh stepped right over him. I'll take you over there sometime if you like. You would love his stories —

RANDOLPH. Wipe that look of interest off your face.

AMANDA. How'm I supposed to tell all that from a picture?

WARREN. Look at the way he's dressed. How many men around here do you see wearing an ascot. *(Warren begins to move around the room. Randolph flinches when he comes near.)* He's got that ... touch of being an actor about him. And if you look in the background there ... see that poster?

AMANDA. *(Honestly excited.)* He was in "Bride of Frankenstein"?

WARREN. *(Nodding.)* Angry villager — *(He picks the sword up from the table.)*

AMANDA. I love that movie.

WARREN. Got to wave a torch and everything. *(Holding the sword.)* He was in *Robin Hood* too. The Errol Flynn version. *(He swings the sword in Randolph's direction.)* That's one of my favorites. *(He thrusts. Randolph lets out a shriek and jumps away. Warren pursues him as he speaks and fences.)* That great scene on the staircase with Basil Rathbone.

RANDOLPH. For God's sake m'love, will you stop that maniac? *(Warren gives one more thrust. Randolph leaps behind Amanda.)*

WARREN. Great movie. Harry was one of the people in the Sherwood Forest. *(He touches the book with the point of the sword.)* See, it's easier than you thought.

RANDOLPH. End this right now!

WARREN. Ready to try again?

AMANDA. No. *(She moves away.)* It's stupid. *(Miriam enters carrying a lit birthday cake.)*

MIRIAM. Happy birthday —

AMANDA. How do I know you're not just making that all up?

WARREN. Well, I'm not. Mailman's honor.

AMANDA. We all know what that's worth, don't we?

MIRIAM. *(Putting down cake.)* Amanda!

RANDOLPH. Go for it! Take no prisoners!

AMANDA. That's what you said today, remember?

WARREN. No.

AMANDA. I had a friend here. And you said you wouldn't say anything — but you ran right down the path and told her. Sure, I'll trust you.

MIRIAM. He did not tell me!

AMANDA. Then how'd you know?

MIRIAM. You left out two champagne glasses — that's how I knew.

RANDOLPH. Uhhh — oh ...

MIRIAM. You'd make a lousy burglar kiddo — you leave clues all over the place.

RANDOLPH. Don't blame me.

MIRIAM. Now I think you owe Warren an apology.

WARREN. Doesn't matter —

MIRIAM. Yes it does! *(To Amanda.)* Well?

RANDOLPH. Don't you dare ...

AMANDA. I'm sorry Warren.

WARREN. It's okay —

AMANDA. No, I really am, I'm sorry. It's just I thought —

WARREN. Apology accepted. And, boy, am I glad that's cleared up. I wouldn't want you to go around thinking I was a snitch or something ...

RANDOLPH. I can't take much more of this — *(For the remainder of the scene, Randolph grows more and more intolerable. Amanda is torn; she tries to listen to Warren and ignore Randolph, who gets increasingly louder.)*

WARREN. Look Amanda, uhh ... well, I know we didn't meet

under the best circumstances ... with, well, my watch and all —
RANDOLPH. Don't you see what he's trying to do —
WARREN. So I uhhh ... I don't expect us to be best friends
right away — *(Randolph moves directly behind Warren, speaking over
his shoulder.)*
RANDOLPH. He wants to marry her!
WARREN. But I think you should know —
RANDOLPH. We don't need him here!
WARREN. That I think a lot of your mom —
RANDOLPH. Fight back!
WARREN. And ... I'm not sayin' that you'll be crazy about
me right away but —
RANDOLPH. He'll be here all the time —
WARREN. But I'd like for you to just ... give me a chance.
RANDOLPH. All the time!
AMANDA. *(To Randolph.)* Shutup!
MIRIAM. *(Pouncing on her.)* What did you say? *(Randolph exits
through the front door. Amanda tries to stop him and explain at the
same time.)*
AMANDA. I wasn't talking to —
MIRIAM. *(Shaking her.)* Get upstairs! Now!
AMANDA. I didn't mean to —
MIRIAM. Did you hear me? *(Randolph heads for the path.
Amanda breaks from Miriam and runs after him.)* Get back here!
*(But Amanda has disappeared down the path after Randolph.
Miriam slams the door shut.)* Damnit! *(She begins to gather her
painting supplies.)* I'm sorry Warren ... I'm sorry this had to
happen.
WARREN. Give her time —
MIRIAM. *(Frustrated.)* Time won't help. Nothing helps —
WARREN. What're you doing?
MIRIAM. She's not the only one that can run away. I can
run away too ya know.
WARREN. Sit down a minute —
MIRIAM. I have to finish your birthday present!
WARREN. Forget my present —
MIRIAM. *(Flustered.)* No. I have to catch the moon tonight ...
I have to ... *(She calms a moment.)* I want it to be right. *(She grabs*

a mining helmet from the shelf and turns on the lamp.)
WARREN. I'll come with you —
MIRIAM. I rather be alone for a little while — *(She steps outside.)*
WARREN. *(Confused.)* What do you want me to do Miriam? Just tell me what you want. *(The phone rings.)*
MIRIAM. Answer the phone. *(She moves away — stops.)* I'm sorry Warren. *(She exits down the path. Warren crosses to the phone.)*
WARREN. Hello Mrs. Simpers ... I just knew it was you ... no, she's not ... no, she's not either ... I don't know when ... Warren Zimmerman ... right, the mailman ... *(He looks down at his birthday cake and blows out the candles.)* Beg your pardon? ... "What am I doing here at this hour?" ... *(He laughs sadly.)* Got me.

THE LIGHTS FADE

SCENE 2

About two hours later. The house is almost completely dark, except for one small lamp. Warren, barely visible, is asleep on the couch. Amanda enters from the path heading for the house. She stops a moment, noticing that it is dark. She moves towards it — uncertain.

AMANDA. Warren? You still here? *(She is about to step into the house when Randolph appears on the path. He is dressed in the ceremonial robes of a samurai warrior. He whistles softly. Amanda quickly steps into the house, her back to the couch.)* Go away.
RANDOLPH. There's a beautiful moon —
AMANDA. I've seen it —
RANDOLPH. Come out and talk to me m'love. *(No response.)* Please. *(She debates a moment, then steps outside.)* Am I forgiven?
AMANDA. He's gone.
RANDOLPH. A new record! That calls for a celebration —

AMANDA. *(A little louder.)* He's gone.

RANDOLPH. So? *(She sits on the steps, saying nothing.)* For God's sake say something, will you? *(Nothing.)* Okay, fine. *(He sits, looking away from her.)* I'm not talking to you either. *(Silence. Finally, he jumps up.)* Say something! I can't stand it when you're like this.

AMANDA. You shouldn't have done that to him.

RANDOLPH. What did I do?

AMANDA. You got me confused ... you made me ... oh, you know what you did.

RANDOLPH. What about what he did to me? He started it.

AMANDA. No. We did. We started it.

RANDOLPH. What did we do to him that was so terrible?

AMANDA. It's what we did to her. *(Silence.)*

RANDOLPH. I didn't do anything that part of you didn't want me to.

AMANDA. Just leave, will you Randolph? She's on her way home.

RANDOLPH. I'll come back when you're calm ...

AMANDA. I am calm. And I don't want you coming back. *(He gives a short, derisive laugh.)* I'm serious. I am.

RANDOLPH. No you're not.

AMANDA. Yes I am! This is ridiculous. I am arguing with you and you don't exist.

RANDOLPH. Maybe. But I dress well.

AMANDA. You don't exist! And I always use you to ... I just ... don't want you here anymore.

RANDOLPH. Then why'd you call me back? *(She says nothing.)* Hmmmmm?

AMANDA. *(A shrug.)* Say good-bye, I guess.

RANDOLPH. *(Moving towards her.)* Listen m'love —

AMANDA. No. Don't start —

RANDOLPH. I'm a part of you m'love — *(She does not respond.)* I can change.

AMANDA. No you can't. *(She moves towards him, softening a little.)* I went over to where she was painting. Try and apologize or something, I don't know. And on the side of the mountain there she looked so ... lonely by herself.

RANDOLPH. Optical illusion. It's a big mountain.

AMANDA. *(Ignoring him.)* And as I got closer I saw she wasn't painting. She was just ... her shoulders were goin' up and down and I ... just watched her till she started packing up.

RANDOLPH. She'll get over it.

AMANDA. That's not the point —

RANDOLPH. Since when —

AMANDA. Since now. We made her cry.

RANDOLPH. Knock off the "we" stuff. I don't exist, remember?

AMANDA. All right, I did it. It was me — I made her cry. And what if I did it all those other times too with Morty and Steve and ... I mean, we just ... I just used to do it. Never thought about ... you know — her. Now he's gone too.

RANDOLPH. Do you really think you'd want to spend a lifetime with *him* hanging around the house.

AMANDA. I don't intend to spend my "lifetime" here. And what if she doesn't find anybody else, hmm? I don't think I want her up here by herself because ... well, she's gonna need somebody to keep an eye on her after I go. I mean ... somebody's gotta remind her to ... pay the phone bill and ... order oil for the furnace and ... my God, could you picture her with a checkbook? ... and ... and she's gonna need somebody and ... I'm just not always gonna be around to keep an eye on her, that's all. And ... she liked him. *(Silence.)* He was better than the others.

RANDOLPH. He's wasn't in our league —

AMANDA. She liked him ... *(She turns away from, heading back to the house.)* I don't need you anymore Randolph. Good-bye.

RANDOLPH. I can't believe I'm being replaced because of an overweight mailman.

AMANDA. *(Quietly.)* Least he was real. And I don't think you're so perfect anymore.

RANDOLPH. I am too.

AMANDA. You acted like a big baby tonight. And you were scared of him. You hid behind me.

RANDOLPH. I'm only scared when you are m'love. *(Moves to her.)* What're you scared of?

AMANDA. *(After a moment.)* Things bein' different, I guess. *(Silence for a moment. He touches her face; she moves away.)* Go away.

RANDOLPH. *(He observes her, unsure.)* This isn't funny anymore m'love. Now, I apologized. Can we please go back to normal? *(She shakes her head. He moves to her — desperate.)* Then what happens to me now? Hmmmm? What? *(Laughs nervously.)* Hey Kiddo, the old line's true. Without you, I'm nothin'.

AMANDA. *(Closing her eyes.)* Please ... go away.

RANDOLPH. Permanently? *(She nods.)* Well, since it's permanent ... you leave me no alternative. *(He kneels, ceremoniously.)*

AMANDA. What're you doing?

RANDOLPH. The honorable thing. *(He pulls out whatever sort of knife those guys use to kill themselves.)*

AMANDA. That's not funny.

RANDOLPH. *(Poised.)* Tell me about it. Two outfits ruined in one night. *(He readies himself.)*

AMANDA. *(Moving towards him.)* Don't.

RANDOLPH. Why not?

AMANDA. Cause I don't want you to —

RANDOLPH. Not to worry, I don't exist. So it's not as if someone will trip over my body — *(He raises the knife.)*

AMANDA. All right, it doesn't have to be permanent.

RANDOLPH. *(Still poised.)* We can meet for a drink occasionally?

AMANDA. Just not for awhile, okay? *(A beat.)*

RANDOLPH. I can live with that. *(He lowers the knife and rises.)*

AMANDA. So, ahh ... well, good-bye. *(She turns for the door.)*

RANDOLPH. Hey! *(She stops.)* I'm always around if you need me. All you have to do is whistle —

AMANDA. *(Holding up her hands.)* I know the rest of it.

RANDOLPH. You'll miss me.

AMANDA. Once in awhile. *(He looks at her for a moment.)*

RANDOLPH. Je t'adore, m'love.

AMANDA. I know. *(He blows her a kiss and exits down the path.*

She stands a moment, watching him go, then turns and enters the house. She crosses towards the stairs when she sees Warren, still sound asleep.) Warren? *(She lets out a little laugh of relief and moves to him. She shakes him gently.)* Warren ... Warren? *(Shakes him a little harder. No reaction.)* Warren? *(He does not wake up, but holds his arms together as if cold. She stands a moment, then crosses for the quilt. She picks it up, runs her hand over it, then crosses to Warren and begins to cover him with it. As she does this, Miriam enters from the path. She carries her supplies and wears her miner's cap. She takes it off and turns out the lamp as Amanda steps out onto the porch. Wary.)* Hi.

MIRIAM.   *(Cool.)* Hi.

AMANDA.   Get it done?

MIRIAM.   No.   *(Glancing around.)* Hello Randolph. *(She moves towards the door.)*

AMANDA.   He's not here.

MIRIAM.   Well, I'll have to take your word for that, won't I. *(She crosses past Amanda into the house. She puts down her painting supplies and does not notice Warren.)*

AMANDA.   He is.   He's gone.

MIRIAM.   That must mean Warren is too. *(She puts down her things and crosses to stairs — stops when she sees Warren. She looks back at Amanda, says nothing, then shakes him gently.)* Warren?

AMANDA.   I already tried that.   He's out. *(Miriam realizes what he's covered with.   She touches the quilt and looks at Amanda. Simply.)* Let's not sell it.

THE LIGHTS FADE

PROPERTY PLOT

Preset

Off-Stage at Top of Stairs

Wet/soapy rag (for Amanda to wipe off water-color paint)
Sofa pillow #1 (for Amanda to throw down the stairs at
    Randolph)
Large man's Timex wrist watch (Amanda brings it down; it is
    Warren's)
Elizabethan dagger (for Randolph in Act Two, Scene 1)
7 volumes of *World Book* encyclopedia (Amanda; volumes A
    through F)

On the Stairs

Runner carpeting
Painting (on wall): "Moon Over the Tree"
Painting (on wall): "Moon Over the Railroad Yard"
Bannister (sturdy enough to stand on)

Up-Right

Small roll-top desk (sturdy enough to stand on)
   on top: empty space to stand on (S.R.)
               framed photo (C.)
               desk lamp with shade (S.L.)
   inside: legal size ledger ring binder (S.R.) with
                  blank check (ready to tear out)
                  ball point pen
                  calculator
               miscellaneous desk dressing (C.)
               desk phone with long cord (to reach sofa, S.L.)
   chair (pushed into desk)
               wine-color shawl with fringe (draped over
                  back of chair)

Up-Center

Painting (on wall): "Moon Over the River"
Wooden easel (collapsable type) with
  title painting (resting on easel): "Moon Over the
  Brewery" with paint-spattered bath towel (attached at top
  and draped over)
Closet rod with
  curtain
  miscellaneous hangers with clothes (waiting to be ironed)
  pink feather boa (stage dressing)

Up-Left

2 wall sconces with mini shades with
  broom stick (hanging between the sconces) with
    Miriam's patchwork quilt (bright colors on navy
    background; it is folded and draped over the
    broomstick)
Ironing board with
  iron
  miscellaneous painting supplies
Painting (on floor under the ironing board): "Moon Over
  the Factory"
Sewing machine (on floor under the ironing board)
Light switch (on wall by kitchen door; starts in the "Up"
  position)
Kitchen door (starts closed) with
  Miriam's note to Amanda written on an envelope (taped
  to door)

Off-Stage in the Kitchen

2 champagne glasses (Amanda)
Can of 7-Up (new each show; Amanda)
Glass of water (Amanda gives to Warren)
Pots and pans (for Randolph to make crashing noise)

Pie-tin (for "Morty the Raccoon") with
  Chinese noodles "leftovers"
Wooden tray (Miriam brings it on) with
    coffee carafe (coffee set is pottery type) with decaf coffee
    3 matching mugs
    matching creamer with milk
    matching sugar bowl with lid, sugar spoon, sugar
    3 spoons
2 paint brushes (for Miriam to enter cleaning) with clean,
  dry dish rag
Large plate with
    birthday cake (homemade look; can be faked since
    never eaten) with 10 lit candles (or more if desired;
    Warren is 44)
Off-stage matches or lighter

Stage-Left

Fireplace mantle with
    framed photo (U.S.)
    miscellaneous painting supplies (C.)
    small fan (C.)
    painting (leaning up against chimney): "Moon Over the
      Junkyard"
    empty area to leave room for candles (D.S.)
Several blank canvases (on floor leaning against fireplace)
Umbrella stand (D.S. of fireplace on floor) with
    umbrella (stage dressing)
    saber (used by Randolph in Act One)
    scabbard (stage dressing)
    paint-spattered yardstick (stage dressing)
Dining chair with padded seat (D.S. of umbrella stand)
Cassette player (old-fashioned piano-board type; wired from
    the sound booth, but wire looks like a regular electric
    power cord) with
        cassette (insider player; labelled "Mozart Horn
        Concerto #3")

Sewing basket (stage dressing) with
    scraps of material
    spools of thread
Small wooden dining table (spattered with paint) with
    2 dining chairs (pushed under the U.S. and
        S.R. sides)
    wooden painter's palette (dried paint, doesn't need to
        be wet)
    several tubes of oil paint (for Miriam to put into her
        "kit")
    several small oil brushes (for Miriam to put into her
        "kit")
    tall clay sculpture (something in progress)
    wooden, hinged art box "kit" with rope handles, with
        tray of damp water-color paints (for Amanda to
            "accidentally" get all over her hands)
        several tubes of oil paints
        several small oil brushes
        1 clean, dry dish cloth (to "clean" brushes with)
        large rubber bands (to bind together easel when
            collapsed)
    miscellaneous painting supplies:
        glass vase with several large brushes
        turpentine can filled with water
        distressed rags
        roll of paper towels
        paint-spattered coffee can
        several plastic cups

Down-Center

Wooden crate filled with
    books (all shapes, sizes, kinds)

Stage-Right

Oval rag rug (under sofa)
Floor lamp (at U.L. corner of sofa) with
    pink, fringed shade

Small sofa (love-seat size) with
   cloth flower-print throw cover
   2 sofa pillows (#2 and #3)

Down-Right

Square ottoman (angled in the corner) with
   pile of newspapers (underneath sticking out)
Sofa pillow (#4; on floor just U.S. of the ottoman)
Small side table (on S.R. "wall") with
   Miriam's miner's helmet with working light (on bottom
      shelf)
   miscellaneous dressing (on top; must be secured to surface
      since Amanda will toss a pillow there to cover up
      Warren's wristwatch)

Porch

Screen door (on spring)
Porch light
Railings (strong enough for Randolph to climb and stand on)

"Outside" Yard

Moon box
Telephone pole with
   "electrical" cables (to the house)
Suspended tree branches
Wooden bench (S.R. of cellar doors; seats two)
Cellar doors (can be sat on) with
   lock and hasp
7-Up cooler (S.L. of cellar doors; can be sat on)
3/4 size garbage can with lid (not too tall for sightlines)
Bucket (stage dressing)
Miscellaneous gardening supplies (stage dressing)
Post with
   attached clothesline (other end attaches to chimney) with
      clothespins on the line (no clothes)
Chain-link fencing

Off-Stage Prop Table

Leather briefcase (Amanda)
Silver cigarette case (Randolph) with
  cigarettes
  matching silver cigarette holder
  matching silver Zippo-type lighter with
    fluid
    flint
Distressed mailman's bag (Warren) with
  cardboard inserts (to keep sides of bag from sagging)
  Cabernet bottle (new, never opened)
  Chablis bottle (new, never opened)
  various junk mail
  flat-type paper store bag with
    paperback book: *The Encyclopedia of Film* ($24.95 on it)
    paperback book: *Shogun*
  medium size photo album with
    20-25 snapshots of people
    1 photo of a beautiful older woman
    1 photo of a distinguished man wearing an ascot
Bicycle (Miriam)
Empty pie tin (identical to the one from the kitchen;
    switched to indicate that "Morty the Raccoon" has eaten
    the leftovers)
Light color ring box (Warren; never opened so no need for a
    ring)
Samurai's dagger (for Randolph in Act Two, Scene 2)

Ready Off-Stage for Intermission

7 mis-matched, lit, votif-type candles (for Miriam)
Off-stage matches or lighter
Tall glass of water (for Amanda)
Opened Chablis bottle (identical to the one in Warren's mail
    bag) with
      water (gets thrown onto Randolph's costume,
        so do not use food coloring or juices as the
        Chablis)

2 wine glasses (for Miriam and Warren) with
  water (as Chablis)
3 tie-dyed cloth napkins
3 plates with
  Chinese noodles
3 sets of chopsticks (fancy colors)
Wok with
  lid, serving spoon, Chinese noodles
Square tablecloth (to spread out on floor)
Canvas cloth (to cover the dining table and painting supplies)

Note: For Act Two, it should look like Miriam and Amanda have covered up and moved the mess, rather than cleaned it up. During intermission, remove both the ironing board and one of the dining chairs into the kitchen. Move the dining table, still covered with paint supplies, to the U.S. wall where the ironing board was. Put one of the dining chairs under the dining table on the S.L. side, and hang Miriam's paint smock on the back of the chair. Cover the table and paints with the canvas cloth, and place 3 lit candles on top (leaving room on the S.L. end for later when the coffee tray sits there). Place 2 more lit candles on the fireplace mantle. Place the tablecloth on the floor, picnic style, where the dining table used to be. Place 1 lit candle in the middle of the tablecloth as a center piece, then set up the wok, plates, flatware, glassware, napkins, chopsticks, and Chablis bottle. Pull out the cassette player and set it next to the picnic area, with its "power cord" (speaker wire) trailing off to the fireplace area. Take the fringed shawl from the back of the roll-top desk chair, and use it to cover up the wooden crate of books; put the last lit candle on top. (Leave room for later when the birthday cake will be set on top of this crate.)

COSTUME PLOT

ACT ONE

Amanda
(based on what a business person would wear, but found at a
  thrift store):
Muted striped man's dress shirt
Brown/white pattern man's tie
Tailored wine color skirt
White socks
Brown leather tie topsiders shoes
Small wristwatch

Randolph
(a cross between a 30's/40's movie idol and a contemporary
  hero, perhaps out of the *Great Gatsby*):
2 piece white linen suit
Wine color striped shirt with a white collar and cuffs
Old-fashioned button suspenders
Original 40's pattern tie with ivory/gold on brown/grey
2 tone dress shoes

Warren
(traditional U.S. Postman's summer uniform):
U.S. Postman's hat
U.S. Postman's light blue short sleeve shirt with insignia
U.S. Postman's blue/grey shorts
Blue knee socks
Black walking shoes

Miriam
(waitress uniform with original/character touches):
Hot pink and black fish earrings
Hot pink funky sunglasses

Worn out white sweater
Pink plastic bracelet
Medium blue waitress uniform (skirt and top)
Hippy-style handbag
Yellow/pink pattern socks
Dirty pale pink sneakers
Moccasins (to change into)

ACT TWO, Scene 1

Amanda
Blue and white striped cotton T-shirt
Straight leg, traditional worn blue jeans
Typical 80's dirty white worn sneakers
Wrist full of tie-on cloth bracelets

Randolph
(a sea-faring man from the 1800s, perhaps out of *Shogun*):
Mustache
Black hooded robe (to assist in making his initial entrance
    unseen)
Wine color wool sleeveless doublet with cord trim
Gold satin period shirt with open neck and full sleeves
Rust-brown color textured breeches
Knee-high leather boots

Warren
Cotton short sleeve shirt with light pink stripes on white
    background
Synthetic dark grey slacks
Pale rose and blue pattern tie
Black belt
Black dress shoes

Miriam
Hot pink 3/4 sleeve cotton knit top
Rayon skirt with hot pink/teal flowered print on black
   background
Nylons
Woven lavender belt
Ethnic silver necklace and earrings
Pink and silver bracelets
Paint smock (when she goes out to paint)

ACT TWO, Scene 2

Randolph
(a Samurai warrior's ceremonial garb, also from *Shogun* per-
   haps):
Generously cut white brocade kimono (worn open)
Dark brown/navy blue brocade silk kimono (worn under-
   neath) and tied with a cord
White Japanese toe socks
Japanese sandals

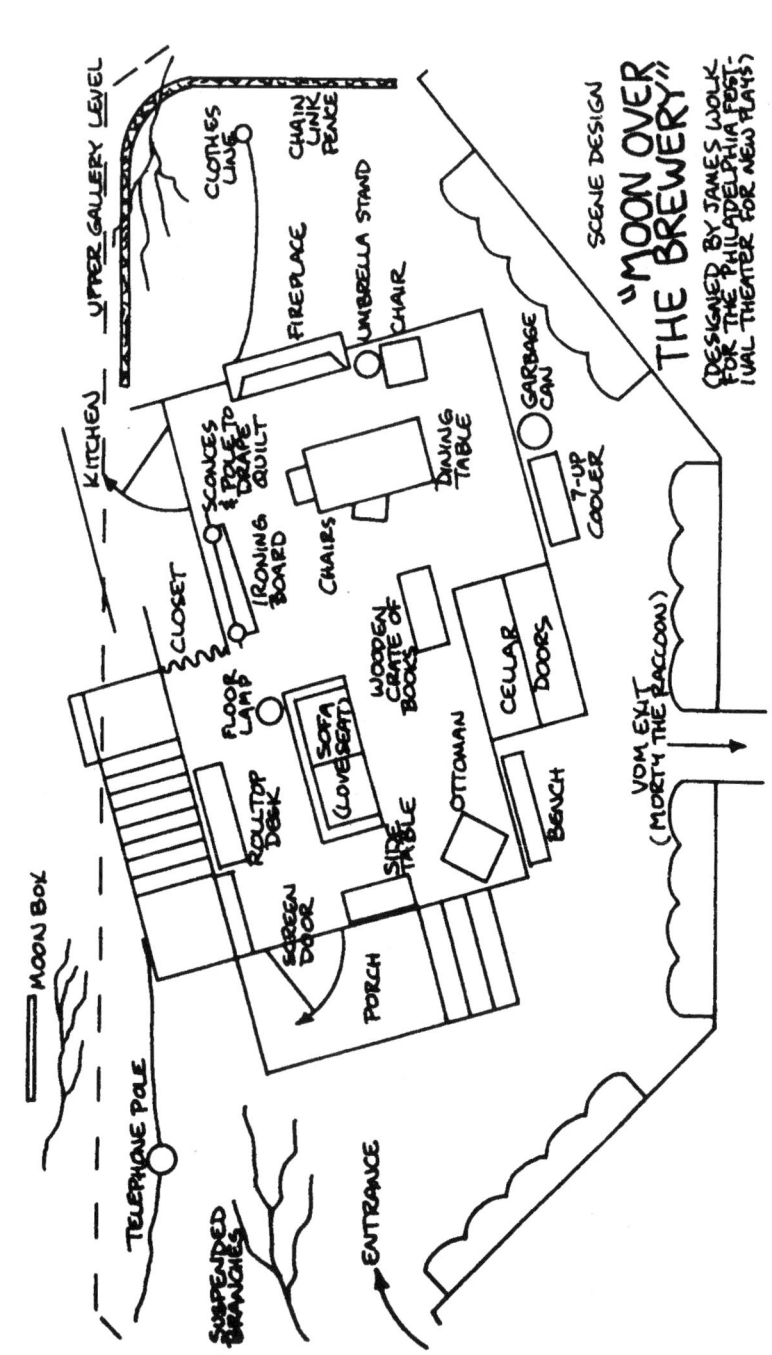

SCENE DESIGN
"MOON OVER THE BREWERY"

(DESIGNED BY JAMES WOLK FOR THE PHILADELPHIA FESTIVAL THEATER FOR NEW PLAYS)

MOON BOX

TELEPHONE POLE

SUSPENDED BRANCHES

ENTRANCE

UPPER GALLERY LEVEL

CLOTHES LINE

CHAIN LINK FENCE

FIREPLACE

UMBRELLA STAND

CHAIR

KITCHEN

SCONCES & PLATE TO DRAPE QUILT

IRONING BOARD

CLOSET

FLOOR LAMP

ROLLTOP DESK

SCREEN DOOR

PORCH

SIDE TABLE

SOFA (LOVESEAT)

OTTOMAN

WOODEN CRATE OF BOOKS

CHAIRS

DINING TABLE

GARBAGE CAN

7-UP COOLER

CELLAR DOORS

BENCH

VOM EXIT (MORTY THE RACCOON)